Nashville CUISINE

Bernie Arnold

Nashville CUISINE

A Sampling of Restaurants & Their Recipes

Compiled and Edited by

BERNIE W. ARNOLD

Two Lane Press

First printing November 1992

ISBN 1-878686-08-9

Printed in the United States of America

Cover design, hand lettering, and text ornaments: Calvert Guthrie
Editing and text design: Jane Doyle Guthrie
Food consultant: Judith Fertig

Two Lane Press, Inc.
4245 Walnut Street
Kansas City, MO 64111
(816) 531-3119

To Bud, who makes it all worthwhile

🏛 Contents

▥ Acknowledgments

A big thanks must go first to the nice people at Two Lane Press, especially editor/cheerleaders Karen Adler and Judith Fertig, for taking a chance on someone who had never written a cookbook.

I'm very grateful to the Nashville chefs and restaurant owners whose response made this book possible, as well as to Al Eady (alias "Big Al"), manager of the Radio Shack on Charlotte Avenue in Nashville, who made house calls when I needed help with my computer.

And I'm especially thankful to my husband, Henry Arnold, who kept the home fires burning.

▣ Introduction

There was a time when the best food in Nashville was served mainly in private homes. Country music fans came to see the Grand Ole Opry, history buffs to view the Parthenon and historic plantations; no one came because of outstanding restaurants. But times have changed. About three decades ago Nashville discovered culinary life beyond the Mason-Dixon line, and a cosmopolitan mix of eateries began to appear on the local scene.

Unlike some towns, such as Kansas City with its beef and Memphis with its barbecue, Nashville didn't have a signature cuisine—unless you count our deep-rooted love for garden-fresh vegetables and super-sweet desserts. Restaurateurs capitalized on this, and many eating establishments evolved into trendy combinations of down-home, haute cuisine, ethnic, and new-style Southern.

Tourists say Nashville is a friendly place, and this includes many restaurant operators. There are waiters who go out of their way to make guests feel welcome, particularly in the unpretentious family-owned diners. Fortunately, the friendliness doesn't end there. If you're persistent, restaurant owners and chefs will share treasured recipes, and the fruits of our persistence appear in the sections that follow in this book.

It takes time to savor Music City. A long vacation here might solve the tourist's dilemma. So would coming down the first weekend in June when Summer Lights, a festival showcasing Nashville's graphic and performing arts, is held on Legislative Plaza. Many restaurants set up food booths. The idea is to stroll from one to the other, eating, listening to music, and watching the performers.

In any event, y'all come.

Bernie W. Arnold

Beginnings

❋ Grilled Tomato and Feta Cheese Salad with Toasted Pecan Vinaigrette

4 medium ripe tomatoes
Olive oil
1 pound mixed greens
　　(arugula, mâche, dandelion,
　　frisée, or your favorite)
1 head radicchio
1/2 pound feta cheese,
　　crumbled

Slice tomatoes 1/4-inch thick. Brush with small amount of olive oil and grill lightly so that the tomatoes remain firm. Arrange tomatoes and greens attractively on a plate, garnishing with radicchio. Sprinkle with feta cheese. When ready to serve, drizzle **Toasted Pecan Vinaigrette** over salad.

Serves 4

Toasted Pecan Vinaigrette

2 tablespoons balsamic vinegar
6 tablespoons olive oil
1 teaspoon honey
4 tablespoons toasted pecan
　　pieces
Salt and pepper to taste

Combine vinegar, oil, and honey in a bowl and whisk lightly. Add pecans, then salt and pepper. Stir just before serving, as dressing will separate. (*Note:* Can be made up to a week in advance. Also goes well with game.)

Makes about 3/4 cup

MERE BULLES
152 Second Avenue North
Nashville, Tennessee 37201
(615) 256-1946

Puffy Muffin Chicken Salad Plate

4 cups cooked and chunked
  chicken breast
1 small can crushed pineapple,
  drained
1 cup finely chopped celery
1-1/2 cups seedless grapes,
  halved
Mayonnaise to moisten

Combine chicken with remaining ingredients. Serve on a bed of lettuce. (*Note:* Can make up to 2 days in advance.)

Serves 4

THE PUFFY MUFFIN
H.G. Hills Shopping Center
231 Franklin Road
Brentwood, Tennessee 37027
(615) 373-2741

❧ Cold Pasta Salad with Vegetables

1 pound spiral-shaped tricolor
  pasta
1 small can pitted olives,
  drained
1 small zucchini, sliced
1 small carrot, sliced
1 small crookneck squash,
  sliced
1 small red onion, sliced
2 medium ripe tomatoes, sliced
2 stalks celery, sliced
2 cups broccoli florets
1 tablespoons oregano
1 teaspoon dill
1/4 cup red wine vinegar
1-1/4 cups virgin olive oil
1/4 cup grated Parmesan
  cheese

Boil pasta until al dente, then drain and cool. Combine with vegetables. Mix herbs with red wine vinegar and olive oil. Pour vinaigrette over pasta and vegetables. Mix well. Top with Parmesan cheese. (*Note:* Can be made 3 to 4 days ahead.)

Serves 12 to 14

MOSKO'S MUNCHEONETTE
2204 Elliston Place
Nashville, Tennessee 37203
(615) 327-3562

❈ Clayton-Blackmon's Greek Salad

2 pounds cucumbers, seeded
    and sliced thickly
1 pint cherry tomatoes,
    stemmed and halved
1 bunch parsley, chopped
1 tablespoon chopped fresh
    oregano (optional)
1 bunch green onions, chopped
    (tops included)
2 red bell peppers, seeded and
    sliced
2 yellow bell peppers, seeded
    and sliced
8 ounces feta cheese, crumbled
1/2 cup pitted and drained
    black olives
2 large cloves garlic, crushed
1 cup extra-virgin olive oil
3/4 cup red wine vinegar
2 tablespoons dried oregano
2 tablespoons Dijon mustard
Salt and freshly ground pepper
    to taste

Combine first 9 ingredients in a large salad bowl. In a blender or food processor, whirl together garlic, olive oil, vinegar, oregano, mustard, salt, and pepper. Pour dressing over salad ingredients, toss, and serve.

Serve with pita bread wedges that have been brushed with olive oil, garlic, and Parmesan cheese.

Serves 8 to 10

CLAYTON-BLACKMON GOURMET DELI AND CATERING COMPANY
4117 Hillsboro Road
Nashville, Tennessee 37215
(615) 297-3441

❋ Asparagus Surprise

1 (7-ounce) poached chicken
    breast, fat, skin, and bones
    removed
1 small egg
1/4 cup heavy cream
6 sprigs watercress
1/2 cup chopped fresh
    broccoli, blanched and
    cooled
12 fresh asparagus spears,
    blanched and cooled
    (reserve 12 asparagus tips for
    garnish)
Salt and pepper to taste
Baby lettuce leaves
Reserved asparagus tips
Cherry tomato halves

In a food processor, blend cooked chicken until smooth. Add egg, cream, watercress, broccoli, asparagus, salt, and pepper. Blend until smooth. Spoon mixture into 4 small timbale molds and steam by covering with foil and placing in a roasting pan. Fill pan with hot water three-fourths up the sides of the molds. Bake in a preheated 350-degree oven for 15 minutes. Cool for 1 hour before removing chicken.

To serve, unmold chicken onto a bed of lettuce and garnish with asparagus tips and cherry tomato halves. Serve with **Vinaigrette Dressing**.

Serves 4

Vinaigrette Dressing

1/4 cup tarragon vinegar
1 tablespoon chopped shallots
2 tablespoons Dijon mustard
1 tablespoon chopped parsley
1 cup olive oil
Salt and pepper to taste

Combine vinegar, shallots, mustard, and parsley, and blend well. Slowly add oil, whisking constantly. Season with salt and pepper. If too strong, add a few drops of water.

Makes about 1-1/2 cups

OLD HICKORY
Opryland Hotel
2800 Opryland Drive
Nashville, Tennessee 37214
(615) 889-1000

❋ Carrot and Dill Soup

4 medium carrots, peeled and
  finely minced
2 tablespoons chopped fresh
  dill
4 tablespoons butter
1 cup rich chicken or duck
  stock
1/2 cup cream

In a medium saucepan, cook minced carrots in butter with dill for 30 to 40 minutes over very low heat. Add stock and simmer for 15 minutes. Cool and refrigerate.

When ready to serve, add cream and heat soup through. Season with salt and pepper.

Serve with a hearty bread.

Serves 4

ARTHUR'S IN UNION STATION
1001 Broadway
Nashville, Tennessee 37203
(615) 255-1494

❧ Minnesota Wild Rice Soup

1/2 cup (heaping) wild rice
1 teaspoon vegetable oil
4 cups water
6 tablespoons butter
1 medium onion, chopped
2/3 cup (scant) or
    10 tablespoons flour
3 cups chicken stock
2 cups half-and-half (or
    whole milk)
Salt and pepper to taste

Sauté rice in oil just to lightly toast. Add water and bring to a boil. Continue cooking until almost done (rice will begin to pop open). Do not overcook. Drain; reserve rice and cooking water in separate bowls.

Melt butter, then add onion and cook slowly until onion is translucent. Add flour and mix well. Cook over low heat, stirring occasionally, for about 10 minutes (do not let mixture brown). Gradually add chicken stock and reserved cooking water from rice. Cook and stir over medium heat until mixture comes to a boil. Add rice and half-and-half. Simmer for about 20 minutes (do not let soup come to a boil).

This hearty soup can be a meal in itself, and is wonderful served with fresh fruit and French bread.

Serves 4 to 5

MERRIDEE'S BREAD BASKET
110 Fourth Avenue South
Franklin, Tennessee 37604
(615) 790-3755

✺ Italian Sausage and Cabbage Soup

1 pound Italian sausage,
  casings removed
1 medium onion, chopped
1 (46-ounce) can V-8 juice
1 small head cabbage, coarsely
  chopped
1 (16-ounce) can white kernel
  corn, undrained
1 teaspoon chili powder
2 teaspoons sugar
1 cup diced peeled potato
1 teaspoon salt
1 (16-ounce) can chili beans
1 (16-ounce) can creamed corn

Brown sausage with onion, then drain fat. Add next 7 ingredients and bring to a boil. Reduce heat and simmer for about 2 hours. Add chili beans and creamed corn, then simmer for 30 minutes more. (*Note:* Best prepared the day before.)

This soup is a very hearty, cold-weather dish. Try it with grilled cheese sandwiches or crusty bread.

Serves 6 to 8

MOSKO'S MUNCHEONETTE
2204 Elliston Place
Nashville, Tennessee 37203
(615) 327-3562

❊ Lemon Chicken Tarragon Soup

2-1/2 cups cooked chicken, cut
    into cubes
6 tablespoons butter
1 cup chopped onions
2 teaspoons minced garlic
3/4 cup flour
5 cups chicken consommé
1 chicken bouillon cube,
    crushed
1 tablespoon finely chopped
    fresh tarragon
Dash of Tabasco sauce
1-1/4 cup heavy cream
1/4 cup fresh lemon juice
Lemon slices
Fresh tarragon leaves

In a saucepan, melt butter. Add onions and garlic, and sauté until translucent. Add flour, mixing well, and cook for 5 minutes. Mix consommé with crushed bouillon cube. Slowly add to flour mixture, stirring well to achieve a smooth texture. Bring to a boil, then reduce heat and simmer for 5 minutes. Add tarragon, Tabasco, cream, and lemon juice. Remove from heat. Add chicken cubes, ladle into bowls, and garnish with lemon slices and tarragon leaves.

Serves 8 to 10

THE SECOND STORY CAFE
Davis-Kidd Booksellers
4007 Hillsboro Road
Nashville, Tennessee 37215
(615) 385-0043

❋ New Potato Soup

1/2 cup (1 stick) butter
2 cups diced onions
1/2 cup flour
3 tablespoons crushed chicken
    bouillon cubes
1/4 cup instant mashed
    potatoes
4 cups warm water
2 cups half-and-half
1 teaspoon chopped basil
    leaves
Dash of Tabasco sauce
3 cups chopped, boiled new
    potatoes
Grated cheddar cheese
Crumbled bacon

Melt butter in a saucepan. Add onions and sauté until soft and translucent, about 10 to 15 minutes. Add flour and stir to blend. Cook for 5 minutes. Dissolve chicken bouillon and instant mashed potatoes in the warm water. Slowly add to flour mixture, whipping to incorporate the liquid. Gradually bring liquid to a simmer and cook for 15 minutes. Add half-and-half, seasonings, and cooked potatoes. Cook for another 5 minutes or until soup is heated through. Garnish with grated cheese and crumbled bacon.

Serves 8 to 10

THE SECOND STORY CAFE
Davis-Kidd Booksellers
4007 Hillsboro Road
Nashville, Tennessee 37215
(615) 385-0043

❁ Potato Soup

6 tablespoons butter or
    margarine
4 cups chopped yellow onion
1 medium carrot, grated
1/2 cup chopped celery
6 chicken bouillon cubes
6 cups chicken broth
6 cups thinly sliced and peeled
    russet potatoes
Salt and pepper to taste
1/4 cup parsley flakes
2 cups heavy cream
Chopped chives or scallions

Melt butter or margarine in a heavy saucepan, and sauté onions, carrot, and celery until translucent. Add bouillon, chicken broth, and potatoes (broth should just cover potatoes). Simmer until vegetables are tender. With an electric mixer or in several batches in a food processor, chop cooked vegetables into tiny pieces (do not puree; potatoes should be coarse and chunky). Add seasoning and cream. Warm through, or serve chilled, topped with chives or scallions. (*Note:* Can be made 1 to 2 days in advance.)

Serves 12 to 14

MOSKO'S MUNCHEONETTE
2204 Elliston Place
Nashville, Tennessee 37203
(615) 327-3562

❈ Tuscan Tomato Soup

2 tablespoons unsalted butter
1/4 cup olive oil
2 carrots, finely minced
2 stalks celery, finely minced
2 medium onions, finely
  minced
10 large ripe tomatoes, skinned
  and seeded
2 teaspoons sugar
2 1/2 quarts water
1/2 cup chopped fresh basil
Salt and pepper to taste
1/2 cup grated Parmesan
  cheese

Heat butter and oil in a large heavy pot. Cook carrots, celery, and onions over medium heat for 20 minutes or until soft. Do not brown. Add tomatoes, sugar, water, and half of the basil. Simmer for 15 to 20 minutes. Stir in remaining basil and season well with salt and pepper. Ladle into bowls and garnish with Parmesan cheese.

Serves 8 to 10

THE PINEAPPLE ROOM
Cheekwood
1200 Forest Park Drive
Nashville, Tennessee 37205
(615) 352-4859

❈ Tomato Basil Soup

4 tablespoons butter
1/4 large onion, chopped
6 large tomatoes, chopped
1 quart tomato juice
1-1/2 teaspoons chopped
    fresh basil
2-1/2 cups chicken broth
1/2 teaspoon pepper
1/2 cup sliced fresh mushrooms
Grated Parmesan cheese
Chopped fresh parsley

In a heavy saucepan, melt butter. Add onions and sauté until clear. Add the next five ingredients and simmer for 45 minutes. Add mushrooms and cook for 15 minutes. Ladle into soup bowls and garnish with Parmesan cheese and chopped parsley. (*Note:* Can be prepared a day ahead. Rewarm when ready to serve.)

Serves 8

THE PICNIC, INC.
4334 Harding Road
Nashville, Tennessee 37205
(615) 297-5398

✻ Fresh Blueberry Soup

1 cup fresh blueberries
Juice of 1/2 lemon
1 cinnamon stick
2 cups water
Pinch of salt
1/4 cup sugar
1 tablespoon cornstarch
2 tablespoons cold water
1/4 cup heavy cream

Simmer blueberries, lemon juice, and cinnamon stick in water until berries are tender, about 15 minutes. Stir in salt and sugar. Mix cornstarch with cold water and stir into blueberry mixture. Bring to a boil, reduce heat, and simmer for 2 minutes. Remove from heat and discard cinnamon stick. Puree blueberries in a blender and chill. (*Note:* Can be made to this point 3 to 4 days in advance.)

Just before serving, stir in cream. Serve in chilled glasses as a first course or frost glass rims with sugar, top mixture with a dollop of whipped cream, and serve as a dessert.

Serves 6

OUR HOUSE
1059 Haley Road
Wartrace, Tennessee 37183
(800) 876-6616

✺ Cheese Wafers

1 pound sharp cheddar cheese,
   grated
1 cup all-purpose flour
3/4 teaspoon cayenne pepper
1/2 cup (1 stick) butter or
   margarine, melted

In a bowl, combine cheese, flour, and cayenne pepper. Pour melted butter over mixture and blend well with hands. Pinch off walnut-sized pieces of dough and roll in hands to form small balls. Place dough pieces on a cookie sheet and bake at 350 degrees for about 18 minutes (dough will flatten as it bakes). (*Note:* Best made only 1 day in advance.)

Wonderful served with cocktails or salads.

Makes about 40 wafers

BIDDLE'S LUNCH BOX
Koger Center, Gatlinburg Building
7101 Executive Center Drive
Brentwood, Tennessee 37027
(615) 370-8565

❧ Pineapple Dip

1 (8-ounce) package cream
    cheese, softened
1 (8-ounce) can crushed
    pineapple, drained
1 tablespoon finely diced onion
1/2 teaspoon garlic salt
Poppy seed crackers

Beat cream cheese until fluffy. Add pineapple, onion, and garlic salt. Chill. Serve with crackers (poppy seeds enhance the flavor of the dip). (*Note:* Can be prepared up to 4 days in advance.)

Serves 6 to 8

THE PUFFY MUFFIN
H.G. Hills Shopping Center
231 Franklin Road
Brentwood, Tennessee 37027
(615) 373-2741

❈ Pimiento Cheese Spread

1 pound American cheese,
  grated
1 cup mayonnaise
1 teaspoon finely chopped
  pimiento

Place all ingredients in a bowl and mix until smooth. Spread on bread slices or crudités. (*Note:* Keeps well for several days.)

Makes about 3 cups

BIDDLE'S LUNCH BOX
Koger Center, Gatlinburg Building
7101 Executive Center Drive
Brentwood, Tennessee 37027
(615) 370-8565

❈ Country Dijon Honey-Mustard Spread

2 cups mayonnaise
1/2 cup country Dijon mustard
  (with seeds)
1/2 cup vegetable oil
2 teaspoons cider vinegar
1/2 cup honey
1/4 teaspoon onion salt

Combine all ingredients and blend well. Chill. Serve on club sandwiches or BLTs, or as a salad dressing.

Makes about 4 cups

BIDDLE'S LUNCH BOX
Koger Center, Gatlinburg Building
7101 Executive Center Drive
Brentwood, Tennessee 37027
(615) 370-8565

❇ Faison's Pâté Maison

2 pounds fresh chicken livers
2 tablespoons chopped onion
9 slices bacon, cooked
1/2 cup cognac
1 cup (2 sticks) butter, melted
  and cooled
1-1/2 teaspoons anchovy paste
2 tablespoons granulated garlic
2 teaspoons dry mustard
1/2 teaspoon nutmeg
1/2 tablespoon rosemary
1/4 teaspoon cloves
1/2 teaspoon cayenne pepper
1 teaspoon salt
Toasted almonds

In just enough water to cover the bottom of the pan, sauté chicken livers and onions until livers are light brown. Drain off liquid. Transfer livers and onions to food processor bowl along with bacon, cognac, butter, and anchovy paste. Process until smooth. Add remaining ingredients except almonds. Process again until thoroughly blended. Chill overnight or up to 24 hours.

Serve at room temperature, garnished with almonds.

Serves 12

FAISON'S
2000 Belcourt Avenue
Nashville, Tennessee 37212
(615) 298-2112

❇ Chopped Liver Pâté

2 pounds calf or baby beef
   liver, sliced and salted
2 pounds onions, sliced
3/4 cup vegetable oil
6 hard-cooked eggs
1 cup chopped celery
1 small onion
Salt and pepper to taste

Bake liver slices in a 350-degree oven, turning once or twice, until no longer pink, about 30 to 40 minutes.

In a 2-quart pot, cook onions in oil over medium heat for 45 minutes or until golden brown. Strain onions, reserving oil.

Skin cooked liver and remove any veins. Cut into pieces. In a food processor or meat grinder, grind or chop liver, eggs, celery, cooked onions, and small raw onion together. Blend well. Gradually add reserved oil, stirring after each addition, until mixture is very soft. Season with salt and pepper, and refrigerate.

Serve with crackers or on cocktail rye bread.

Serves 12

SCHWARTZ'S DELICATESSEN
Belle Meade Plaza
Harding Road
Nashville, Tennessee 37205
(615) 292-3589

❊ Chicken Liver Turnovers

1 pound chicken livers
All-purpose flour
Salt and pepper to taste
1/4 cup (1/2 stick) butter, plus
    additional melted to brush
    on pie dough
1/4 cup chopped onions
1/8 teaspoon A-1 Sauce
Pastry dough for double-crust
    pie
Grated Parmesan cheese
Paprika

Dust chicken livers with flour. Sauté in butter with onions and A-1 Sauce. Season with salt and pepper. Remove from heat, chop, and set aside.

Preheat oven to 350 degrees. Roll out pastry dough and cut into 2-inch rounds. Put a teaspoon of the meat mixture on half of a round; fold over other half. Press edges together with the tines of a fork. Brush pastry with melted butter, and sprinkle with Parmesan cheese and paprika. Bake for about 20 to 30 minutes or until light brown. (*Note:* Turnovers can be frozen before baking.) Serve hot.

Makes 60 turnovers

SATSUMA TEA ROOM
417 Union Street
Nashville, Tennessee 37219
(615) 256-0760

❈ Quail Stuffed with Raspberry Barley in Port Wine and Ginger Sauce

4 semiboneless quail
1 tablespoon diced onion
1 tablespoon diced carrot
1 tablespoon diced celery
1 tablespoon vegetable oil
2 cups cooked barley
1 pint fresh raspberries
   (reserve several for garnish)
1 tablespoon honey
Salt and pepper to taste
2 tablespoons butter, divided
1 tablespoon sour cream or
   yogurt (optional)
4 sprigs lemon thyme

Preheat oven to 350 degrees. Sauté onion, carrot, and celery in oil until soft. Add to cooked barley. Add raspberries, honey, salt, and pepper. Mix lightly, being careful not to mash the berries. Stuff quail from the leg end, trying not to break the skin. Tie legs together with cotton twine. Place stuffed quail breast-side up on a lightly buttered pan. Melt butter and brush quail lightly. Season with additional salt and pepper. Bake for 15 to 20 minutes, until quail are golden brown and crisp.

To serve, pour 1/4 cup of **Port Wine and Ginger Sauce** in the center of 4 plates. Remove twine and place a bird in the center of each plate. With a toothpick, swirl sour cream or yogurt through sauce. Garnish with reserved raspberries and lemon thyme sprigs.

Serves 4

Port Wine and Ginger Sauce

1 teaspoon diced fresh ginger
2 tablespoons butter (plus
   additional if desired)
1 cup ruby port
1 cup chicken or beef broth

Stir diced ginger and butter in a saucepan over medium-high heat for 3 to 5 minutes. Add wine and broth. Cook to reduce to syrup-like consistency. Whisk in additional butter if desired.

Makes about 1 cup

MERE BULLES
152 Second Avenue North
Nashville, Tennessee 37201
(615) 256-1946

Smoked Nova Scotia Salmon with Garnish

12 thin slices smoked salmon
3 Boston lettuce leaves, rinsed
3 tablespoons capers, drained
1/2 red onion, finely chopped
1 (8-ounce) package cream
  cheese, quartered
4 slices white bread, toasted
  and quartered into triangles
Unsalted butter
1 lemon, cut into wedges
Dill sprig

Arrange lettuce leaves on an attractive serving plate. Place capers in the center of 1 leaf, chopped onion in the second, and pieces of cream cheese in the third.

Butter 12 cooled toast triangles. Roll each salmon slice in the shape of a rose and place on a toast point (butter will help keep salmon in place). Arrange toast points with salmon "roses" around edges of serving plate. Garnish with lemon wedges and dill sprig.

Serves 4

RHETT'S
Opryland Hotel
2800 Opryland Drive
Nashville, Tennessee 37214
(615) 889-1000

Jubilee Shrimp

12 large shrimp, peeled and deveined, tails intact
1-1/2 cups heavy cream
4 tablespoons unsalted clarified butter
4 medium shallots, minced
6 tablespoons Jack Daniel's whiskey
Salt and freshly ground white pepper to taste
Minced fresh parsley

In a heavy saucepan over medium heat, simmer cream until reduced by half. In large heavy skillet, melt clarified butter over medium-high heat. (*Note:* To clarify butter, melt in a heavy saucepan over low heat. Skim froth from surface, then carefully pour clear yellow liquid into another dish, leaving milky residue in pan. Discard residue.) Add shrimp and cook until just opaque, about 1 minute on each side. Remove shrimp from skillet. Stir in shallots and sauté until soft, about 2 minutes (do not brown).

Remove pan from heat and drain off butter. Pour whiskey into a corner of the skillet and heat. Carefully ignite, shaking pan gently until flames subside. Add reduced cream and simmer until reduced by a third. Season with salt and pepper. Return shrimp to skillet and heat thoroughly. Divide among heated plates, sprinkle with minced parsley, and serve warm.

Serves 4

MISS MARY BOBO'S BOARDING HOUSE
Main Street
Lynchburg, Tennessee 37352
(615) 759-7394

✺ BBQ Shrimp

24 jumbo shrimp, peeled and
    deveined
8 sticks (2 pounds) butter
2 tablespoons dried basil
4 teaspoons pepper
2 teaspoon cayenne pepper
1 teaspoon salt
Juice of 1 lemon
2 teaspoons Tabasco sauce

Melt butter in a sauté pan. Add remaining ingredients except for shrimp and cook together for a few minutes. For flavors to develop, allow to stand for at least 1 hour.

When ready to serve, reheat sauce and add shrimp. Sauté until shrimp turn pink.

Serve with French bread to mop up the delicious sauce!

Serves 4

12TH & PORTER
114 12th Avenue North
Nashville, Tennessee 37203
(615) 254-7236

✺ Seafood Rémoulade

1/2 teaspoon salt
1/2 teaspoon cracked pepper
1/2 teaspoon paprika
2 tablespoons anchovy paste
2 tablespoons tomato catsup
4 tablespoons fresh lemon
 juice
4 tablespoons vinegar
4 tablespoons horseradish
4 tablespoons Creole mustard
1/2 cup finely minced celery
 with leaves
1/2 cup finely minced green
 onions
1 cup vegetable oil
3 pounds jumbo shrimp or
 lobster, freshly boiled
Assorted fresh greens (endive
 or leaf, Boston, or Bibb
 lettuce)
Peeled, sliced tomatoes
Sliced oranges

Place salt, pepper, paprika, anchovy paste, catsup, lemon juice, vinegar, horseradish, Creole mustard, celery, and green onions in a mixing bowl. Whisk well while adding oil in a thin stream. Refrigerate. Serve over cold, freshly boiled seafood, arranged on a bed of greens and garnished with peeled, sliced tomato and orange slices. (*Note:* Rémoulade can be prepared the day before.)
Serves 6

HACHLAND HILL INN
1601 Madison Street
Clarksville, Tennessee 37043
(615) 647-1400

✺ Treasure of the Sea

12 medium shrimp, peeled and
    deveined
12 scallops
4 puff pastry shells, frozen
8 mushrooms, sliced
2 tablespoons chopped shallot
1/2 cup sherry
2 cups heavy cream
Salt and pepper to taste
2 tablespoons chopped parsley

Preheat oven to 350 degrees. Bake puff pastry shells for 12 to 14 minutes or until browned and puffed.

In a sauté pan, sauté shrimp, scallops, and mushrooms. Add shallots and sherry to pan, and deglaze by cooking over high heat, scraping bottom of pan to loosen drippings into the liquid. Add heavy cream and reduce by half. Season with salt and pepper, then add chopped parsley. Spoon mixture into puff pastry shells, arrange each shell on a heated plate, and serve.

Serves 4

CASCADES
Opryland Hotel
2800 Opryland Drive
Nashville, Tennessee 37214
(615) 889-1000

✺ Belon Oysters in Sauce Sauterne

24 fresh Belon oysters (or any
  good oyster), shucked
  (reserve half the shells)
3 shallots, finely chopped
1/2 cup sauterne wine
1 cup heavy cream
1 pound spinach leaves, rinsed
  and patted dry
1 tablespoon unsalted butter
4 large egg yolks
1/4 cup whipped cream

Preheat the grill or broiler. Place oysters, together with their liquor, in a non-aluminum saucepan. Add shallots and wine. Cook oysters over medium heat for 3 minutes. With a slotted spoon, remove oysters from pan and keep warm. Boil liquid remaining in pan until reduced to 2 tablespoons. Add heavy cream and boil until reduced to 1/2 cup.

In a pot large enough to hold the spinach, melt butter. Add spinach and sauté over high heat for 4 minutes. Drain. Place 6 oyster shells on each of 4 gratin dishes. Divide the spinach evenly among the shells, pressing in lightly. Top with an oyster; spoon sauterne sauce over each. Beat egg yolks lightly and fold into whipped cream. Place a spoonful of the mixture on each oyster and broil until lightly browned. Serve immediately.

Serves 4

JULIAN'S RESTAURANT FRANÇAIS
formerly at
2412 West End Avenue
Nashville, Tennessee

❋ Baked Oysters with Crabmeat and Pesto

24 oysters, shucked and rinsed
1 cup jumbo lump crabmeat

Preheat oven to 350 degrees. Place about
1 teaspoon of crabmeat on each oyster. Add
1 teaspoon of **Pesto** on top of crabmeat.
Place oysters in a pie pan and bake for 3 to
5 minutes or until desired doneness is
achieved.

Serves 4

Pesto

1 cup pine nuts
2 tablespoons minced garlic
3/4 cup firmly packed fresh
   basil
1-1/2 cups olive oil
1/4 cup plus 2 tablespoons
   grated Parmesan cheese

In a food processor, puree pine nuts,
garlic, and basil until smooth. Gradually
add olive oil in a thin stream until mixture
thickens. Add Parmesan and mix well. Set
aside.

Makes about 3 cups

PLAZA GRILLE
Loew's Vanderbilt Plaza Hotel
2100 West End Avenue
Nashville, Tennessee 37203
(615) 320-1700

⬛ Mussels Marinara

48 mussels
1/2 cup olive oil
4 teaspoons minced garlic
2 cups diced tomatoes
2 cups tomato sauce
4 tablespoons chopped green
 onions
1 cup dry white wine
4 teaspoons fresh lemon juice
1 teaspoon dried oregano
1 teaspoon dried basil
1 teaspoon pepper
1 teaspoon red pepper flakes
1 teaspoon salt

Scrub mussels with a brush under cold water; remove beards. Heat oil in large pan and add garlic, cooking until it becomes golden but not brown. Add mussels, tomatoes, tomato sauce, green onions, wine, lemon juice, and spices. Cook for 5 to 7 minutes or until mussels open. (Discard any that do not open.) Serve immediately with sauce.

Serves 4

CAESAR'S RISTORANTE ITALIANO
Lion's Head Village
88 White Bridge Road
Nashville, Tennessee 37205
(615) 352-3661

❈ Deep-Fried Calamari with Rémoulade Sauce

2 pounds fresh calamari
    (smallest tubes possible),
    cleaned and diced into 1-
    inch pieces
1 cup milk
3 cups cake flour
Vegetable oil
Salt
Lemon wedges

Soak calamari in milk for 2 minutes. Drain and dredge in flour; shake off excess. Heat oil to 375 to 400 degrees and deep-fry calamari until golden. Season with salt. Serve with **Rémoulade Sauce** and lemon wedges on the side.

Serves 6

Rémoulade Sauce

1/2 cup mayonnaise
1 tablespoon drained and
    chopped capers
1 teaspoon chopped
    cornichons (tiny pickles)
1 teaspoon hot Dijon mustard
1 tablespoon chopped fresh
    basil
1 tablespoon chopped fresh dill
1 tablespoon chopped fresh
    tarragon
1 tablespoon chopped fresh
    cilantro
2 tablespoons red wine vinegar
1/4 teaspoon white pepper
1/4 teaspoon cayenne pepper

Mix all ingredients and whirl until smooth in a food processor.

Makes about 3/4 cup

F. SCOTT'S
2220 Bandywood Drive
Nashville, Tennessee 37215
(615) 269-5861

Crab Rangoon

1/2 (8-ounce) package cream cheese, softened
2 tablespoons crabmeat
1 green onion, chopped
1/4 teaspoon pepper
8 wonton skins
4 cups vegetable oil

Combine cream cheese, crab, and onion, then add pepper. Divide mixture evenly among wonton skins, putting mixture in center of each wonton. Bring corners together securely to hold filling inside. In a heavy saucepan, heat oil until hot. Deep-fry wontons until golden brown.

Serves 6

PEKING GARDEN
1923 Division Street
Nashville, Tennessee 37203
(615) 327-2020

❁ Conch Fritters

1-1/2 pounds conch meat
   (or chopped clams)
1 large yellow onion, cubed
3 bell peppers, cubed
1/2 stalk celery, cubed
7 eggs
4 cups self-rising flour
1 teaspoon salt
4 tablespoons garlic powder
3/4 teaspoon black pepper
3/4 teaspoon cayenne pepper
1 teaspoon white pepper
Vegetable oil

In food processor, grind seafood and vegetables together; set aside. In a mixing bowl, combine eggs, flour, and seasonings until just incorporated. Fold in seafood mixture. (Do not overmix or fritters will be tough.) Heat oil in a fryer or skillet. Drop batter by heaping tablespoons into oil and cook until browned, approximately 3 minutes. Remove from oil and drain on paper towels.

Serve these with cocktail sauce or chutney.

Makes about 100 bite-sized appetizers

RAINBOW KEY
Lion's Head Village
80 White Bridge Road
Nashville, Tennessee 37205
(615) 352-7252

❂ Corn Fritters with Red Pepper Jelly

1 (20-ounce) package frozen
    corn kernels, cooked and
    drained
3 eggs, beaten
1-1/4 cups finely chopped
    white onion
1/4 cup chopped shallots
1/2 teaspoon finely minced
    garlic
2-1/2 tablespoons finely
    chopped cilantro
1-1/2 cups all-purpose flour
1/2 cup cornmeal
1-1/2 tablespoons salt
1 tablespoon sugar
1-1/2 tablespoons baking
    powder
1-1/2 tablespoons ground
    coriander
1/2 teaspoon pepper
Vegetable oil

Puree corn in a food processor, then beat in the eggs. Add chopped onions, shallots, garlic, and cilantro to corn mixture. In a separate bowl, combine remaining dry ingredients. Fold the two mixtures together thoroughly. (*Note:* Batter will remain good for 3 days in the refrigerator.) When ready to fry, heat oil to 350 degrees. Spoon fritter batter into the hot oil and fry until deep golden brown. Remove from oil and drain on paper towels. Serve warm with **Red Pepper Jelly.**

Makes 30 to 40 fritters

Red Pepper Jelly

3 red bell peppers, seeded and
    diced
6 jalapeño peppers, seeded and
    diced
1/2 cup cider vinegar
2 cups sugar
1 package fruit pectin

Puree peppers in a food processor, then mix with vinegar and sugar in a saucepan. Boil mixture for 10 minutes. Add pectin, stir, and boil for 1 minute more. Remove from heat, pour into sterile jars, and allow to cool to room temperature.

Makes 3 cups

BELLE MEADE BRASSERIE
101 Page Road
Nashville, Tennessee 37205
(615) 356-5450

❊ Spinach Fritters

1 pound frozen chopped
   spinach, thawed, drained,
   and squeezed dry
2 eggs
1/2 cup bread crumbs
1/2 cup grated Parmesan
   cheese, plus additional to
   garnish
1/2 teaspoon grated nutmeg
1 teaspoon salt
1/2 teaspoon pepper
Vegetable oil

Combine all ingredients except oil. Mixture should be moist and hold together. Form into 1-1/2-inch balls.

In a deep fryer or electric skillet, heat oil to 350 degrees. Fry dough balls, turning frequently, for about 5 minutes or until lightly browned. Remove fritters from oil, drain on paper towels, then transfer to a serving plate. Sprinkle with additional freshly grated Parmesan cheese and serve warm.

Makes 20 fritters

FINEZZA
5404 Harding Road
Nashville, Tennessee 37205
(615) 356-9398

✹ Fried Tomatoes Stuffed with Boursin

6 large tomatoes
All-purpose flour
2 eggs, beaten
1-1/2 cups cracker crumbs
Vegetable oil

Slice tomatoes to yield 16 slices, about 1/3-inch thick. Spread a 1/2-inch layer of **Homemade Boursin** on 8 tomato slices and top with remaining slices to form 8 sandwiches. Refrigerate until cheese is firm.

Dip each chilled tomato sandwich first in flour, then beaten eggs, then cracker crumbs. Refrigerate again to set coating.

To serve, fry tomato sandwiches in 1/2 inch of oil (or deep-fry). Serve immediately as an appetizer or as a vegetable accompaniment.

Serves 4 to 6

Homemade Boursin

1 (8-ounce) package cream
   cheese, softened
1/3 cup sour cream
1/4 cup (1/2 stick) butter,
   softened
1 large clove garlic, minced
1 tablespoon snipped chives
1 tablespoon snipped parsley
1/4 teaspoon dried thyme
1/8 teaspoon pepper

Combine ingredients until well blended.

Makes about 2 cups

CHOICES RESTAURANT
108 Fourth Avenue South
Franklin, Tennessee 37064
(615) 791-0001

Main Courses

Angel Hair St. Andrew

4 tablespoons olive oil
4 tablespoons chopped fresh
   basil
4 tablespoons diced fresh garlic
8 cups fresh plum tomatoes,
   peeled, seeded, and chopped
12 ounces spinach angel hair
   pasta, cooked
12 ounces egg angel hair pasta,
   cooked
1/2 teaspoon white pepper
4 tablespoons freshly grated
   Parmesan cheese
Salt to taste

Heat oil in a medium skillet. Add basil and garlic, and cook until tender (do not brown garlic). Add tomatoes and bring to a boil. Reduce heat to low, and simmer for 5 minutes. Add pasta and pepper. Stir until thoroughly heated. Season with salt, transfer to a serving bowl, and top with Parmesan.

Serve with a small green salad, Italian bread, and a glass of Chardonnay.

Serves 4

9/3/93: Very good. Cut pasta to 8 oz. max for two (4 oz spinach; 4 oz egg). I used regular tomatoes, which took quite a while to reduce. Otherwise this is fairly quick.

SUNSET GRILL
2001 Belcourt Avenue
Nashville, Tennessee 37212
(615) 386-3663

⚏ Spinach Lasagna with Marinara Sauce

1 pound whole wheat lasagna,
    cooked
1/2 cup sliced artichoke hearts
1 pound fresh spinach,
    steamed
1 cup grated Parmesan cheese
2 cups chopped tofu

Preheat oven to 350 degrees. In a 9-by-13-inch baking dish, pour a ladleful of Marinara Sauce. Layer a fourth of the lasagna noodles on top of the sauce, then a third of the artichoke hearts. Top artichoke hearts with a third of the spinach, then a fourth of the Parmesan, then a third of the tofu. Repeat process twice more, ending with a layer of noodles topped with sauce and Parmesan. (*Note:* May be prepared ahead to this point.) Bake for 45 to 60 minutes or until the sauce bubbles.

Serves 8

Marinara Sauce

3 tablespoons olive oil
1-1/2 cups chopped onions
2 green bell peppers, chopped
1 cup sliced mushrooms
1 (32-ounce) can diced
    tomatoes
1/2 cup water
1/2 cup tomato paste
Pinch of salt
2 tablespoons minced parsley
2 tablespoons chopped fresh
    basil
1/2 teaspoon pepper
1/2 cup dry red wine
1 tablespoon minced garlic

Sauté onions and green peppers in oil for 5 minutes or until onions are translucent. Add remaining ingredients and simmer for several hours, stirring frequently. Serve over pasta.

Makes about 6 cups

SLICE OF LIFE
1811 Division Street
Nashville, Tennessee 37203
(615) 329-2525

12 Caesar's Ziti alla Carbonara

Very good!
9/7/93
+ w/ fusilli
Cut butter in ½
Quite Rich.

8 ounces ziti (hollow, tubular pasta), cooked al dente and drained
6 tablespoons butter or margarine
1-1/2 cups heavy cream
1 cup chopped ham
1 pound fresh asparagus tips or 1 (10-ounce) package frozen, cooked
Salt and pepper to taste
1 cup freshly grated Parmesan cheese
Freshly grated nutmeg

Melt butter in a frying pan over medium-high heat. Add cream, ham, and asparagus. Increase heat to high and cook until liquid comes to a full boil and forms shiny bubbles; reduce heat. Add ziti to sauce, then Parmesan cheese. Mix gently so pasta is thoroughly coated. Dust with freshly grated nutmeg and serve.

Serves 4 to 6

CAESAR'S RISTORANTE ITALIANO
Lion's Head Village
88 White Bridge Road
Nashville, Tennessee 37205
(615) 352-3661

⚂ Pasta Ya Ya

4 tablespoons butter or
   margarine
4 garlic cloves, crushed
1/2 cup chopped green onions
4 boneless, skinless chicken
   breast halves, diced
3/4 pound pork sausage,
   cooked and drained
2 cups chicken stock
1 pound fresh pasta (any style),
   cooked
1 cup heavy cream

In a sauté pan, melt butter or margarine
and sauté garlic and green onions for 1
minute. Add chicken and cook until
chicken begins to turn white. Add sausage,
chicken stock, and pasta. Simmer for 2
minutes. Add cream and reduce for 1
minute. When ingredients have heated
through, mix 4 tablespoons of **Blackening
Spice Mixture** into pasta and serve.

Serves 4

Blackening Spice Mixture

8 tablespoons paprika
2 tablespoons granulated garlic
2 tablespoons onion powder
1-1/2 teaspoons dried thyme
1 tablespoon dried oregano
3-1/2 tablespoons salt
1-1/2 tablespoons black pepper
1-1/2 tablespoons white pepper
1 tablespoon cayenne pepper
1 tablespoon dried basil

Combine all ingredients and store in a
tightly covered jar.

Makes about 2 cups

12TH & PORTER
114 12th Avenue North
Nashville, Tennessee 37203
(615) 254-7236

ⓩ Pasta Mad Platter

3 tablespoons olive oil
1 large onion, julienned
12 mushrooms, sliced
4 artichoke hearts, quartered
8 slices sun-dried tomatoes
16 slices chorizo (Spanish
    sausage), casings removed
1 teaspoon minced garlic
Large pinch of whole dried
    oregano
3–4 cups fresh spinach leaves,
    rinsed and patted dry
1 pound linguine (citrus lemon,
    red pepper, curry, or plain),
    cooked al dente and drained
Montrachet cheese to taste,
    crumbled
Green onions split into
    "brushes" (optional)

Sauté onion in olive oil until soft. Add mushrooms and continue sautéing until mushrooms change color. All at once, add artichoke hearts, tomatoes, sausage, garlic, and oregano. Sauté until warmed through, but not dry. (*Note:* Can be prepared ahead to this point.) Add spinach and sauté until wilted. Reheat pasta by immersing briefly in hot water and draining well. Top with spinach mixture and garnish with Montrachet cheese and green onion brushes.

Serve with a salad of greens and crusty bread.

Serves 4

THE MAD PLATTER
1239 Sixth Avenue North
Nashville, Tennessee 37208
(615) 242-2563

⚄ Broken-Hearted Fettuccine

1/2 cup (1 stick) butter or
    margarine
4 tablespoons chopped garlic
4 tablespoons chopped green
    onions
1/2 pound bay scallops
2 cups heavy cream
1 (6-ounce) can cooked
    crabmeat
1 pound fettuccine, cooked
8 canned artichoke hearts,
    halved
Juice of 2 lemons
Equal parts salt, pepper, and
    granulated garlic to taste

Melt butter or margarine in a sauté pan. Add garlic and green onions, and sauté for 1 minute. Add scallops and cook for 1 minute more. Add cream and simmer for 2 minutes to reduce. Add crab, fettuccine, and artichokes. Toss all together until hot and cream is thick enough to coat pasta. Add lemon juice, salt, pepper, and granulated garlic. Serve immediately.

Serves 4

FAISON'S
2000 Belcourt Avenue
Nashville, Tennessee 37212
(615) 298-2112

⟨2⟩ Black Linguine with Mussels

32 mussels
1 pound black (calamari)
   linguine, cooked, rinsed, and
   drained
1/4 cup extra-virgin olive oil
4 tablespoons minced shallots
1 tablespoon minced garlic
1/2 cup dry white wine
1 cup clam juice
1 red bell pepper, medium dice
Minced parsley
Grated Parmesan cheese

Scrub mussels with a brush under cold water and remove beards. Set aside.

In a large skillet over medium heat, combine olive oil, shallots, and garlic. Sauté briefly to soften, then add wine and clam juice. Bring mixture to a boil, then add mussels and cover skillet. Simmer for 5 minutes until mussels start to open. Discard any mussels that do not open. Arrange mussels on each of 4 plates.

Add linguine to remaining stock in bottom of skillet. Toss in bell pepper. Heat until pasta has absorbed liquid and all ingredients are hot, about 3 to 4 minutes. Divide pasta among plates. Garnish each with a touch of minced parsley and grated Parmesan cheese. Serve immediately.

Try this with an Italian Pinot Grigio or Pescevino wine.

Serves 4

FINEZZA
5404 Harding Road
Nashville, Tennessee 37205
(615) 356-9398

⌐ Crawfish Étouffé

1 pound crawfish tails (with
   fat), cooked (found in
   specialty seafood section of
   grocery)
6 tablespoons butter
2 tablespoons finely diced
   celery
2 tablespoons finely diced
   onion
2 tablespoons finely diced bell
   pepper
2 whole tomatoes, peeled and
   diced
1/2 teaspoon salt
1/2 teaspoon granulated garlic
1/4 teaspoon dried thyme
1/4 teaspoon dried oregano
1/4 teaspoon dried basil
1/4 teaspoon dried rosemary
6 tablespoons all-purpose flour
2 tablespoons finely diced
   green onions
2 tablespoons finely diced
   fresh parsley
2-1/2 cups chicken, shrimp, or
   fish stock
2 tablespoons heavy cream

In a saucepan, melt butter and sauté
celery, onion, and bell pepper. Add
tomatoes, salt, garlic, and herbs. Continue
to sauté over medium heat until vegetables
are translucent, about 15 to 20 minutes.
Stir in flour and mix well. Add green onions
and parsley. Slowly add stock, then cream,
stirring constantly. Add crawfish and
simmer for 10 minutes more. (*Note:*
Prepare in advance, if desired; dish reheats
well in microwave.)

*Serve over hot rice, such as Louisiana
popcorn rice, and garnish with chopped
Italian parsley.*

Serves 6

THE CORNER MARKET
Westgate Shopping Center
6051 Highway 100
Nashville, Tennessee 37205
(615) 352-6772

⚓ Shrimp Scampi

3/4 cup (1-1/2 sticks) butter
2 tablespoons vegetable oil
2 tablespoons minced green
   onion
1 pound mushrooms, sliced
4 teaspoons fresh lemon juice
48 medium shrimp, peeled and
   deveined
2 teaspoons chopped garlic
1/2 teaspoon dried oregano or
   to taste
1/2 teaspoon dried basil or to
   taste
1–2 bay leaves or to taste
1/2 teaspoon dried rosemary or
   to taste
1-1/2 cup Marsala wine
1/2 teaspoon grated lemon zest
Lemon wedges
Chopped fresh parsley

In a wide frying pan, melt butter over medium heat. Add oil, green onion, mushrooms, and lemon juice, and cook until bubbly. Add shrimp, garlic, and dry seasonings to pan. Cook, stirring occasionally, until shrimp turn pink. Add wine and lemon zest. Continue to cook until liquid is reduced by half. Garnish with lemon wedges and chopped parsley.

Serves 4 to 6

CAESAR'S RISTORANTE ITALIANO
Lion's Head Village
88 White Bridge Road
Nashville, Tennessee 37205
(615) 352-3661

❷ Deep-Fried Prawns

48 prawns (about 2 pounds),
   peeled and deveined
3 teaspoons salt
1 teaspoon pepper
1 cup rice wine
8 egg whites
4 tablespoons cornstarch
4 teaspoons all-purpose flour
Vegetable oil
Tomato slices
Lettuce leaves

In a large bowl, combine 2 teaspoons salt, pepper, and wine. Add prawns and allow to marinate for 30 minutes, turning frequently to coat prawns with mixture.

Beat egg whites briefly and set aside. Combine cornstarch, flour, and remaining teaspoon of salt. Dust prawns with cornstarch mixture, then dip into beaten egg whites. Deep-fry in hot oil (320 degrees) for about 2 minutes. Arrange prawns on plates and garnish with tomato slices and lettuce.

Serves 4

DYNASTY RESTAURANT
3415 West End Avenue
Nashville, Tennessee 37203
(615) 269-0188

🗹 Jumbo Scampi

20 jumbo shrimp, peeled and
    deveined
6 plum tomatoes, peeled,
    seeded, and diced
2 tablespoons finely chopped
    garlic
2 tablespoons chopped fresh
    basil
1/4 cup olive oil
Kosher salt to taste
Freshly ground pepper to taste
1/4 cup dry white wine
1 pound angel hair pasta,
    cooked just before serving

Mix tomatoes, garlic, basil, 2 tablespoons olive oil, salt, and pepper. Let mixture marinate for 1 hour.

Heat a large sauté pan. Add remaining olive oil and shrimp, sautéing until shrimp turn pink. Add wine and reduce liquid by half. Add tomato mixture and bring to a boil. Add cooked pasta and toss. Adjust salt and pepper to taste. Divide pasta among 4 plates and arrange shrimp on top. Pour sauce remaining in pan over pasta and serve.

Serves 4

OLD HICKORY
Opryland Hotel
2800 Opryland Drive
Nashville, Tennessee 37214
(615) 889-1000

◪ Creole Shrimp

2 pounds freshly cooked
   medium shrimp, peeled and
   deveined
1 large onion, chopped
1 cup celery, diced
1 green bell pepper, chopped
1 clove garlic, chopped
2 tablespoons vegetable oil
1 (29-ounce) can tomato puree
1 (29-ounce) can tomatoes
1/4 cup firmly packed brown
   sugar
1 teaspoon salt
1/4 teaspoon pepper
Few drops of Tabasco sauce
4 cups hot cooked rice

Sauté onion, celery, bell pepper, and garlic in oil until tender. Add tomato puree, tomatoes, brown sugar, and seasonings. Simmer for 40 minutes. (If time permits, longer, slower cooking of sauce is desirable.) Add shrimp and cook for 10 minutes more. Serve over hot rice. (*Note:* Can be made ahead and reheated.)

This shrimp goes well with a tossed salad and hot homemade rolls. Pass extra Tabasco sauce at the table.

Serves 8

SATSUMA TEA ROOM
417 Union Street
Nashville, Tennessee 37219
(615) 256-0760

▣ Bahama-Que Shrimp

1 pound medium shrimp,
  peeled and deveined
1/2 cup (1 stick) butter or
  margarine, melted
1/2 cup vegetable oil
1 quart chili sauce
1/2 cup Worcestershire sauce
1/2 cup fresh lemon juice
1 tablespoon paprika
1-1/4 tablespoons fresh
  rosemary or 2 teaspoons
  dried
1/4 teaspoon salt
1 tablespoon pepper
1 tablespoon cayenne pepper
1 tablespoon chopped fresh
  oregano or 2 teaspoons dried
1-1/2 tablespoons chopped
  garlic

Place melted butter in a mixing bowl. Add remaining ingredients in the order listed. Blend together until oil is thoroughly incorporated and sauce is smooth. In a skillet or sauté pan, heat sauce until bubbly. Add shrimp and cook for approximately 2-1/2 minutes or until shrimp curl.

Serve with toast points or French bread to soak up the wonderful sauce.

Serves 4 to 6

RAINBOW KEY
Lion's Head Village
80 White Bridge Road
Nashville, Tennessee 37205
(615) 352-7252

⎘ Spinach Seafood Bake

1 pound small shrimp, peeled
  and deveined
1 pound scallops
1 (10-ounce package) frozen
  chopped spinach, thawed,
  drained, and squeezed dry
2 cups artichoke hearts
1-1/2 cups mayonnaise
1-1/2 cups sour cream
1/2 cup grated Romano cheese
1/2 cup ricotta cheese
1/2 cup shredded mozzarella
3 teaspoons chopped garlic
Bread crumbs
Minced parsley

Preheat oven to 350 degrees. Sauté shrimp, scallops, and spinach in a lightly greased pan for 10 to 12 minutes. Chop artichoke hearts and combine with mayonnaise, sour cream, cheeses, and garlic. Mix gently to prevent tearing scallops. Distribute mixture among 8 to 10 gratin dishes. (*Note:* Can be made a day in advance if wrapped tightly with plastic wrap and refrigerated.) When ready to serve, top each portion with bread crumbs and bake for 8 to 10 minutes, until light golden brown. Garnish with chopped parsley and serve.

Serves 8 to 10

32ND AVENUE BRASSERIE
3201 West End Avenue
Nashville, Tennessee 37203
(615) 383-0926

Sea Scallops with Wild Mushrooms

2 pounds large sea scallops
1 pound wild mushrooms
   (shiitake, chanterelles, or
   cèpes)
2 shallots, minced
1/2 cup dry white wine
2 tablespoons fresh lemon
   juice
1/2 cup heavy cream
1 cup (2 sticks) butter, softened
Salt and white pepper to taste
3 tablespoons olive oil
Coarse sea salt
Freshly ground black pepper

Preheat oven to 400 degrees. Quickly rinse mushrooms under cold water, dry well with paper towels, and slice. Set aside.

In a small saucepan, combine shallots, wine, and lemon juice. Bring to a boil over high heat until almost all liquid has evaporated. Add cream and reduce mixture further by half. Remove from heat and whisk in butter, 2 tablespoons at a time. Set aside and keep warm.

Arrange scallops on a lightly buttered baking sheet and sprinkle with salt and white pepper. Bake until scallops just whiten and start to lose their opalescence, about 6 to 8 minutes. Meanwhile, sauté mushrooms in olive oil over high heat until lightly browned, about 4 minutes. To assemble, spoon sauce onto 4 heated dinner plates, sprinkle with mushrooms, and top with scallops. Sprinkle with sea salt and a grind of fresh black pepper. Serve immediately.

Serves 4

BELLE MEADE BRASSERIE
101 Page Road
Nashville, Tennessee 37205
(615) 356-5450

🖂 Scallops en Casserole

2 pounds large sea scallops
3/4 cup (1-1/2 sticks) butter
1/4 cup all-purpose flour
2 cups half-and-half
1/2 teaspoon white pepper
1-1/2 cups grated Swiss cheese
1/4 cup sherry
1/2 cup dry white wine
1/4 cup minced onion
1/2 pound fresh mushrooms,
  quartered
4 slices cooked bacon,
  crumbled
1/4 cup freshly grated
  Parmesan cheese

Over medium-low heat, melt 1/4 cup butter and blend in flour to make a roux. Heat half-and-half in the top of a double boiler and whisk into roux until thickened. Remove from heat and stir in white pepper, Swiss cheese, and sherry. Set aside.

In a sauté pan, melt remaining 1/2 cup butter and add white wine. Sauté onion, mushrooms, and scallops in butter mixture until done, about 5 to 8 minutes (do not overcook). Mix in heated sauce and pour combination into a large shallow casserole dish. Sprinkle crumbled bacon and Parmesan cheese over the top, brown under the broiler, and serve.

Serves 6

MIDTOWN CAFE
102 19th Avenue South
Nashville, Tennessee 37215
(615) 320-7176

⚏ Citrus Grilled Tuna

6 tuna steaks, 1-1/2 inches
   thick
3 cups vegetable oil
1 cup soy sauce
Juice of 1 orange
Juice of 1 lemon
Juice of 1 lime
2 bay leaves
1/4 teaspoon pepper
1 tablespoon fennel seed
6 cloves garlic, crushed
1 tablespoon chopped fresh
   basil
1 teaspoon dried thyme

Whisk together oil and soy sauce. Stir in juices and seasonings.

Let mixture rest for 15 minutes to let flavors blend, then pour over tuna steaks and marinate at room temperature for 10 to 15 minutes (longer, if kept in the refrigerator).

Remove fish from marinade and grill over medium coals for 8 to 10 minutes (4 to 5 minutes per side). Serve immediately.

Serves 6

OUR HOUSE
1059 Haley Road
Wartrace, Tennessee 37183
(800) 876-6616

⌨ Grilled Swordfish in Ginger-Soy Sauce with Dijon Vegetables and Spoon Rolls

6 (6-ounce) swordfish steaks
1 teaspoon minced fresh or
  granulated garlic
2 tablespoons soy sauce
2 teaspoons sherry
2 tablespoons vegetable oil
1 tablespoon sugar
1 tablespoon minced fresh
  ginger or 1 teaspoon
  powdered

Place a single layer of swordfish steaks in a shallow pan. Combine remaining ingredients and pour over steaks. Marinate for a minimum of 2 hours in the refrigerator.

Preheat oven to 350 degrees. Remove fish from marinade and bake for 15 to 20 minutes, depending on thickness of steaks, until done but not dry. (*Note:* May also be grilled or broiled.) Serve with **Dijon Vegetables** and **Spoon Rolls**.

Serves 6

Dijon Vegetables

1 pound green beans, ends
  removed
1 pound carrots, cut into 1/2-
  inch pieces
1-1/2 pounds russet potatoes,
  peeled and cut into 1-1/2-
  inch cubes
1/8 teaspoon freshly ground
  pepper
2/3 cup olive oil
1/3 cup Dijon mustard
1/2 green and 1/2 red bell
  pepper, julienned (optional)

Steam or boil each of the 3 vegetables in separate containers until soft to the bite (do not overcook). Drain vegetables and cool.

Mix pepper, oil, and mustard until blended, then pour over cooked vegetables. Add green and red bell peppers and stir gently. Serve at room temperature.

Serves 6 to 8

Spoon Rolls

1 package dry yeast
2 cups warm water (110 degrees)
1/4 cup vegetable oil
1/2 cup (1 stick) butter or margarine, melted and cooled slightly
4 cups self-rising flour
1/4 cup sugar
2 eggs

Preheat oven to 400 degrees. Dissolve yeast in warm water. In large bowl of electric mixer, combine yeast mixture with remaining ingredients. Mix well until blended. (*Note:* Batter keeps well up to 3 days in the refrigerator.) When ready to serve, spoon batter into small greased muffin tins and bake for 15 to 20 minutes.

Try flavored varieties of these basic rolls by adding one or more of the following: grated sharp cheddar and dill weed; chopped onion; toasted crushed coriander seeds; whole dill seed; or toasted sesame seeds.

Makes 4 dozen

CHOICES RESTAURANT
108 Fourth Avenue South
Franklin, Tennessee 37064
(615) 791-0001

▣ Skillet-Roasted Salmon with Spinach Sauté

4 (6-ounce) salmon fillets
1 pound fresh spinach leaves,
   rinsed and patted dry
1 teaspoon minced garlic
2 tablespoons minced shallots
6 tablespoons butter
Salt and pepper to taste
Lemon wedges or slices

Chop spinach leaves coarsely, and lightly salt salmon fillets. Preheat the broiler. In a large skillet, melt 2 tablespoons butter over medium heat. Lightly sauté salmon fillets in butter for 1 minute on each side, then place under the broiler for 5 minutes.

While salmon is broiling, heat remaining 4 tablespoons butter in a large skillet. Before butter browns, add garlic and shallots. Stir briefly and allow to sauté for 30 seconds. Add chopped spinach leaves, season with salt and pepper, and stir well. Just as the spinach wilts, remove from heat. Divide among 4 plates and top each with a salmon fillet. Garnish with lemon wedges or slices.

Serves 4

BELLE MEADE BRASSERIE
101 Page Road
Nashville, Tennessee 37205
(615) 356-5450

⚜ Salmon Loaf with Cucumber Dressing

1 (16-ounce) can salmon,
    drained and flaked
1/2 cup mayonnaise
1 (10-3/4-ounce) can cream of
    mushroom soup
3 eggs, beaten
1 cup dry bread crumbs
1/2 cup chopped onion
1/4 cup chopped bell pepper
1/4 cup chopped celery
1 teaspoon fresh lemon juice
1 teaspoon salt

Combine all ingredients and pour into a greased loaf pan. Bake at 350 degrees for 1 hour. Slice and serve with **Cucumber Dressing.**

Serves 8

Cucumber Dressing

1/4 cup mayonnaise
1/2 cup sour cream
1/4 cup chopped cucumber

Combine all ingredients and refrigerate until ready to serve.

Makes 1 cup

OUR HOUSE
1059 Haley Road
Wartrace, Tennessee 37183
(800) 876-6616

⏸ Grouper in Corn Husks with Corn Relish and Poblano Cream Sauce

6 (6–7-ounce) grouper fillets
Husks from 2 ears of fresh corn
1 cup olive oil
1 tablespoon minced garlic
1/4 cup chopped fresh cilantro

Mix olive oil, garlic, and cilantro in a bowl. Dip fillets in olive oil mixture. Place a layer of fillets in a glass dish followed by a layer of husks dipped in oil mixture. Repeat layering of grouper and corn husks until all are used. Cover and marinate for 12 to 24 hours.

Preheat oven to 400 degrees. Remove and discard corn husks. Place grouper in a hot skillet and brown for 2 minutes. Finish in oven, 10 to 12 minutes. Transfer fillets to a serving plate and top with **Poblano Cream Sauce**. Serve chilled **Corn Relish** on the side.

Serves 6

Poblano Cream Sauce

1 poblano pepper, roasted and
   peeled
2 cups heavy cream
1/2 cup (1 stick) butter, cut into
   pieces

Combine poblano pepper and cream in a heavy saucepan. Cook over medium heat until mixture is reduced by half. Strain and return to simmer over low heat. Whisk in butter pieces. Keep warm until ready to serve.

Makes about 1-1/2 cups

Corn Relish

2 ears fresh corn, husked
1 medium tomato, peeled,
    seeded, and diced
1 jalapeño pepper, chopped
Juice of 1 lime
1 teaspoon cracked pepper
1/2 teaspoon salt
1 tablespoon olive oil

Roast corn in the oven or on the grill; remove kernels with a knife. Combine corn kernels with diced tomato, jalapeño pepper, lime juice, pepper, salt, and olive oil. Refrigerate for 3 hours, turning every hour.

Makes about 2 cups

MERCHANTS
401 Broadway
Nashville, Tennessee 37203
(615) 254-1892

⬛ Baked Ocean Perch

2 pounds ocean perch fillets
4 onions, sliced
2 cups boiling salted water
1 cup bread crumbs
1/4 cup mayonnaise
1/2 cup sour cream
1 teaspoon Worcestershire
  sauce
1 tablespoon fresh lemon juice
1/4 cup grated Parmesan
  cheese
2 tablespoons chopped fresh
  parsley

Cook sliced onions in salted water until tender. Drain. Spread onions in shallow baking dish just large enough to hold fillets in a single layer. Dredge fillets in crumbs and arrange on top of onions. Combine remaining ingredients and spread over fish. Bake at 350 degrees for 30 to 40 minutes.

Serves 6

OUR HOUSE
1059 Haley Road
Wartrace, Tennessee 67183
(800) 876-6616

◪ Filet of Red Snapper Dieppoise

4 (6-ounce) red snapper fillets
Salt and pepper to taste
All-purpose flour
1/4 cup clarified butter
  (see instructions on p. 26)
2 large shallots, finely chopped
4 wild mushrooms, sliced
4 domestic mushrooms, sliced
1/4 pound (about 1/2 cup) bay
  shrimp, peeled and deveined
8 mussels, scrubbed and
  debearded
1/2 cup dry white wine
3/4 cup heavy cream

Salt and pepper snapper, then dredge in flour, shaking off excess. Place fish in a sauté pan with clarified butter and sauté until light brown. Transfer fillets to a baking sheet and bake in a 350-degree oven for 5 minutes to finish cooking.

While fish is in the oven, add shallots, mushrooms, mussels (in their shells), and shrimp to the same sauté pan. Sauté until mixed well. Add white wine and deglaze pan by cooking over high heat, scraping bottom of pan to loosen dripping into the liquid. When mixture is reduced by half, add cream. Reduce to a sauce consistency and adjust seasonings to taste. Discard any mussels that have not opened. Remove fillets from oven, and equally distribute sauce over the fish.

Serves 4

OLD HICKORY
Opryland Hotel
2800 Opryland Drive
Nashville, Tennessee 37214
(615) 889-1000

Cherokee Forest Rainbow Trout with Mushrooms and Shrimp

4 (8-ounce) fully dressed
  rainbow trout
1/2 cup all-purpose flour
8 tablespoons (1 stick) butter,
  cut into pats and softened
1 tablespoon chopped shallots
12 large mushrooms, quartered
1/2 cup dry white wine
8 large shrimp, peeled and
  deveined
Lemon wedges
Dill sprigs

Lightly flour trout, dusting off excess. In a large sauté pan over medium heat, melt 1 tablespoon butter. Add all 4 trout to pan and lightly brown on one side. Add another tablespoon of butter and repeat process with other side. When trout are browned on both sides, remove to a plate.

Add another tablespoon of butter to pan and sauté shallots and mushrooms until tender. Add wine and shrimp. Cook and reduce liquid by a third. Remove pan from heat and stir mixture to cool a little. Add remaining butter a tablespoon at a time until all is added. Top trout with sauce and place 2 shrimp and 8 mushroom pieces on each fillet. Garnish with lemon wedges and dill sprigs.

Serves 4

RHETT'S
Opryland Hotel
2800 Opryland Drive
Nashville, Tennessee 37214
(615) 889-1000

⒔ Tea-Smoked Frog Legs

12 pairs frog legs
1 cup firmly packed brown
    sugar
2 cups uncooked white rice
1 cinnamon stick
6 pieces star anise
2 cups Chinese black tea leaves
Chinese mustard or plum
    sauce, for dipping

On an elevated wire rack in a large stockpot or vegetable steamer, steam frog legs over boiling water for 1 minute. Remove from heat and allow to cool.

Line a heavy-gauge pot generously with aluminum foil and distribute rice evenly over bottom. Sprinkle brown sugar over the top of the rice. Break cinnamon stick and toss randomly along with star anise over mixture. Last, distribute tea leaves evenly over all. Place frog legs on a rack and position inside pot, leaving a 2-inch gap between rice mixture and rack.

Place pan over high flame until mixture starts to smoke. Reduce heat to medium and cover with aluminum foil. Allow to smoke for 2 to 5 minutes, checking occasionally until frog legs turn golden. Discard smoking mixture immediately (it permeates the house). Cool and refrigerate frog legs until ready to serve, then reheat in a moderate oven. Serve dipping sauces, such as mustard and plum sauce, on the side.

Serves 4

ARTHUR'S IN UNION STATION
1001 Broadway
Nashville, Tennessee 37203
(615) 255-1494

⛝ Marinated Chicken with Honey-Lime Yogurt Sauce

4 boneless, skinless chicken
  breasts
Juice of 1/2 lime (reserve zest
  and remaining 1/2 lime for
  sauce below)
Grated zest of 1 additional lime
1/4 cup soy sauce
3/4 cup dry white wine
2 tablespoons grated fresh
  ginger
Lime wedges

Place chicken breasts in a flat dish.
Combine remaining ingredients and pour
over meat. Marinate for 1 hour in the
refrigerator.

Grill chicken over high heat until done,
about 4 to 5 minutes. To serve, slice at an
angle, fan across plate, and garnish with
lime wedges. Serve with **Honey-Lime
Yogurt Sauce**.

Serves 4

Honey-Lime Yogurt Sauce

1 cup plain yogurt
Juice of 1/2 lime
Grated zest of 1 lime
Honey to taste

Combine all ingredients and serve
alongside marinated grilled chicken
breasts.

Makes about 1-1/4 cups

THE MAD PLATTER
1239 Sixth Avenue North
Nashville, Tennessee 37208
(615) 242-2563

Bridge House Chicken Casserole

2 cups diced cooked chicken
1 (10-3/4-ounce) can cream of
  mushroom soup
3/4 cup mayonnaise
1 cup finely diced celery
1 cup cooked white rice (cook
  in chicken broth)
1 tablespoon fresh lemon juice
1 tablespoon grated onion
1 (4-ounce) can mushrooms
  (optional)
1/4 cup (1/2 stick) butter,
  melted
1/2 cup slivered almonds
1 cup corn flake crumbs

Preheat oven to 350 degrees. Combine first 8 ingredients and spoon into a 9-by-13-inch baking dish. In a small bowl, mix together butter, almonds, and corn flake crumbs, then spread mixture over casserole. Bake for 30 to 40 minutes, cool slightly, and serve.

Serves 8 to 10

BRIDGE HOUSE TEA ROOM
136 North Fourth Avenue
Franklin, Tennessee 37064
(615) 794-7794

⚂ Lemon Chicken with August Moon Fried Rice

8 boneless, skinless chicken
   breast halves
2 teaspoons salt
1/2 cup rice wine
4 egg whites
1 teaspoon white pepper
1/4 cup vegetable oil
1/4 cup fresh lemon juice
1/4 cup firmly packed brown
   sugar
3 tablespoons cornstarch
4 lemons, thinly sliced

Combine salt, 1/4 cup rice wine, egg whites, and white pepper. Marinate chicken breasts in mixture for 20 to 30 minutes.

Remove chicken from marinade, heat oil in wok or pan, and fry chicken for 2 to 3 minutes on both sides. Add lemon juice, sugar, and remaining 1/4 cup wine. Cover and let simmer for 2 to 3 minutes. Stir in cornstarch and cook to thicken sauce. Add lemon slices and simmer for another 2 to 3 minutes. Serve immediately with **August Moon Fried Rice**.

Serves 4

August Moon Fried Rice

2 (4-ounce) boneless, skinless
  chicken breast halves
12 medium shrimp, peeled and
  deveined
1-1/4 teaspoons salt
2 teaspoons rice wine
1 egg white
Dash of white pepper
1–2 eggs, beaten lightly and
  cooked omelet style
1 tablespoon vegetable oil
1 small yellow onion, finely
  chopped
1/4 cup frozen peas
1/4 cup frozen carrots
3 green onions, finely chopped
  (tops included)
1/4 cup bean sprouts
6 cups cooked white rice
2 tablespoons soy sauce

Combine 1/2 teaspoon salt, rice wine, egg white, and white pepper. Marinate chicken and shrimp in mixture for 20 to 30 minutes. Meanwhile, shred cooked eggs and set aside.

Chop chicken into pieces; leave shrimp whole. Heat oil in wok and add chicken, shrimp, yellow onion, peas, and carrots. Stir for 2 to 3 minutes until chicken and shrimp have cooked. Add green onions, egg shreds, and sprouts. Stir in cooked rice, 3/4 teaspoon salt, soy sauce, and pepper, and cook for 2 to 3 minutes more. Serve warm.

Serves 4

AUGUST MOON
Green Hills Court
4000 Hillsboro Road
Nashville, Tennessee 37215
(615) 298-9999

⬚ Chicken Calypso

4 (7-ounce) chicken breasts
1/4 cup flour
Salt and pepper to taste
2 tablespoons clarified butter
  (see instructions on p. 26)
3/4 cup Chablis wine
1 tablespoon shallots, minced
1 papaya, seeded and diced
1/4 cup sugar
1/8 cup raspberry vinegar
1 cup chicken stock
Cayenne pepper to taste
1/2 cup toasted pecans

Dredge chicken in flour seasoned with salt and pepper. Sauté breasts in clarified butter, turning over once. Deglaze pan with 1/4 cup Chablis by cooking over high heat, scraping bottom of pan to loosen drippings into the liquid. Remove chicken and keep warm.

While chicken is warming, make sauce by sautéing shallots and papaya in liquid left in sauté pan. Deglaze pan again with remaining 1/2 cup Chablis. Add sugar, vinegar, chicken stock, salt, pepper, and cayenne pepper. Allow to simmer for 30 minutes, then puree mixture in food processor. Top chicken breasts with sauce and toasted pecans, and serve.

Serve with seasoned rice and a vegetable medley.

Serves 4

CASCADES
Opryland Hotel
2800 Opryland Drive
Nashville, Tennessee 37214
(615) 889-1000

☑ Honey-Lemon Chicken

4 (5–7-ounce) boneless,
  skinless chicken breasts
4 ounces clarified butter (see
  instructions on p. 26)
6 tablespoons honey
4 tablespoons chopped walnuts
2 lemons
1/2 cup all-purpose flour
Parsley sprigs
Lemon wedges

In a sauté pan, heat clarified butter over medium-high heat and sauté chicken breasts for approximately 2 minutes per side. (Chicken should be cooked, but not dry, and appear white all the way through.) Add honey and walnuts. Squeeze juice from both lemons over tops of chicken. Flip breasts once again to coat both sides. Place chicken on a serving plate and scrape remaining honey, walnuts, and lemon juice on top of each breast. Garnish with parsley and lemon wedges, and serve immediately.

This dish goes well with steamed rice and mixed steamed vegetables.

Serves 4

GRANITE FALLS RESTAURANT
2000 Broadway
Nashville, Tennessee 37203
(615) 327-9250

▣ Chicken Breast alla Caesar

4 (6-ounce) boneless, skinless
  chicken breasts
1/2 cup flour
4 tablespoons butter
4 teaspoons olive oil
4 cups sliced mushrooms
4 tablespoons chopped green
  onion
8 thin slices ham
8 thin slices mozzarella or
  Fontina cheese
1 cup dry vermouth
2 cups heavy cream
1 teaspoon dried oregano
1 teaspoon nutmeg
1 teaspoon dried rosemary
1 teaspoon pepper

Pound chicken out thinly. Cut breasts into halves and dust with flour. In a frying pan, melt butter and oil. Sauté chicken on both sides, then add mushrooms and green onions. Place ham and cheese on top of chicken breasts. Add vermouth, cream, and spices to pan. Allow to simmer for 2 minutes, then serve at once.

Serves 4

CAESAR'S RISTORANTE ITALIANO
Lion's Head Village
88 White Bridge Road
Nashville, Tennessee 37205
(615) 352-3661

Peking Garden Chicken with Lemon Sauce

4 skinless chicken breast
   halves, trimmed of fat
1/2 teaspoon salt
1/2 teaspoon pepper
4 egg whites, divided
3 cups vegetable oil
1/2 cup cornstarch
1/2 cup all-purpose flour

Combine salt, pepper, and 2 egg whites. Cover chicken with mixture and allow to marinate for 20 minutes.

In a heavy skillet, heat oil until very hot. While oil is heating, combine cornstarch and flour. Coat chicken with remaining egg whites, then cornstarch and flour mixture. Deep-fry in hot oil until golden brown. Transfer to a serving platter and top with **Lemon Sauce.**

Serve with steamed broccoli and rice.

Serves 4

Lemon Sauce

2 teaspoons butter
1/2 cup water
1/2 cup fresh lemon juice
4 tablespoons sugar

Heat butter in a saucepan. Combine water, lemon juice, and sugar, and add to butter. Allow to boil and thicken.

Makes about 1 cup

PEKING GARDEN
1923 Division Street
Nashville, Tennessee 37203
(615) 327-2020

◪ Herbed Baked Chicken Breast

4 (6-ounce) boneless, skinless
  chicken breasts
1 cup Grey Poupon or Dijon
  mustard
1 cup good-quality mayonnaise
1 cup (2 sticks) unsalted butter,
  melted
1 (8-ounce) package herbed
  bread crumbs
Parsley sprigs

Preheat oven to 325 degrees. Combine mustard, mayonnaise, and butter. Dip chicken breasts in mixture, coating both sides. Roll breasts in bread crumbs until a generous amount coats chicken. Place in a single layer in an oven-proof baking dish. Bake uncovered for 45 minutes. Garnish with fresh parsley and serve. (*Note:* Can be prepared ahead and served cold.)

This goes well with a fresh vegetable vinaigrette salad.

Serves 4

THE PICNIC, INC.
4334 Harding Road
Nashville, Tennessee 37205
(615) 297-5398

☑ Midtown Chicken with Mustard Caper Sauce

4 (6-ounce) skinless chicken
   breasts
1 teaspoon Grey Poupon
   mustard, divided
4 slices prosciutto, quartered
4 paper-thin slices provolone
   cheese, quartered
2 teaspoons grated Parmesan
   cheese, divided
1 egg
1/4 cup half-and-half
1/2 cup all-purpose flour
Vegetable oil

Preheat oven to 250 degrees. Cut a lengthwise pocket along rib edge of each chicken breast. Coat inside of pocket with approximately 1/4 teaspoon mustard. Stuff prosciutto and cheeses inside pockets and press closed. Make an egg wash by mixing egg and half-and-half. Dredge chicken breasts in flour, then egg wash. Place in a roasting pan, cover with aluminum foil, and bake for 45 minutes. Remove chicken from oven and refrigerate.

When ready to serve, heat vegetable oil and deep-fry chicken for 2 minutes, or until browned. Top each serving with 1 tablespoon of **Mustard Caper Sauce** and offer additional sauce at the table.

Serves 4

Mustard Caper Sauce

2 tablespoons butter
2 tablespoons all-purpose flour
4 tablespoons Grey Poupon
   mustard
1 cup milk
3 tablespoons sugar
Pinch of dry mustard
1/2 teaspoon chopped garlic
2 tablespoons capers

Heat butter until melted. Stir in flour and cook mixture over low heat until smooth and well blended. In another saucepan, heat remaining ingredients together. Add butter and flour mixture and whisk to blend. Stir over medium heat until slightly thickened.

Makes about 2 cups

MIDTOWN CAFE
102 19th Avenue South
Nashville, Tennessee 37215
(615) 320-7176

⒓ Coq au Vin with Herbs

6 (6-ounce) skinless chicken
  breasts, halved
1/2 teaspoon dry mustard
1/2 teaspoon onion or garlic
  powder
1/2 teaspoon dried basil
1/2 teaspoon dried sage
1/2 teaspoon dried oregano
1 cup hot water
1 cup sherry
6 cups hot white rice (cook
  using half water and half
  orange juice)
2 tablespoons cornstarch
3 tablespoons water
Red pepper strips
Parsley sprigs

Place chicken breasts in a large baking pan (do not crowd) and sprinkle with dry seasonings. Add hot water and sherry. Cover with foil and bake in a 350-degree oven for 1 hour. (*Note:* Can be prepared ahead to this point and refrigerated until ready to serve.)

When ready to serve, reheat chicken. Remove from baking dish and arrange around the edge of a serving dish. Fill center of dish with hot rice. Dissolve cornstarch in water and stir into chicken juices remaining in baking dish. Cook over low heat until thickened. Pour sauce over rice and chicken, then garnish with red pepper strips and fresh parsley.

Serve with steamed fresh asparagus, topped by a swirl of black olive slices.

Serves 6

HACHLAND HILL INN
1601 Madison Street
Clarksville, Tennessee 37043
(615) 647-1400

⟨2⟩ Intoxicated Chicken

1 (2-1/2 to 3-pound) chicken,
   cut into pieces (or 4 split
   chicken breasts)
Salt and pepper to taste
2 tablespoons butter
2 tablespoons vegetable oil
1/2 cup Jack Daniel's whiskey
6 shallots, chopped
1/4 teaspoon powdered thyme
1/4 cup minced fresh parsley
1/4 cup water
1 cup heavy cream

Sprinkle chicken with salt and pepper. In a large skillet, heat butter and oil. Add chicken pieces and brown on both sides. Add whiskey and carefully ignite, shaking skillet until flames go out. Add shallots and cook for 1 minute. Stir in thyme, parsley, and water, then cover skillet and cook over low heat, turning occasionally, for 25 to 35 minutes. Transfer chicken to a warm platter. Add cream to skillet and simmer, stirring until sauce thickens. Pour sauce over chicken and serve. (*Note:* Entire dish can be made ahead and reheated.)

Serve this creamy creation with a crunchy rice.

Serves 4

MISS MARY BOBO'S BOARDING HOUSE
Main Street
Lynchburg, Tennessee 37352
(615) 759-7394

🄲 Chicken Jerusalem

8 chicken breast halves
1 cup plus 2 tablespoons all-
   purpose flour
1 teaspoon garlic salt
1 teaspoon dried dill
1/4 cup vegetable oil
2 tablespoons butter
2–3 cups half-and-half
1 tablespoon Dijon mustard
1 (16-ounce) can artichoke
   hearts, drained and
   quartered

Combine 1 cup flour with garlic salt and dill. Dredge chicken breasts in seasoned flour. Heat oil and fry chicken until golden brown, about 15 minutes or until done. Pour off oil, reserving crusty particles in bottom of pan. Add butter and remaining 2 tablespoons unseasoned flour to pan. Stir and cook over medium heat until smooth and bubbly. Slowly add half-and-half until mixture is the consistency of pancake batter. Add Dijon mustard and artichokes. When heated through and thickened, serve over chicken.

Rice provides the perfect accompaniment to this dish.

Serves 4

THE PUFFY MUFFIN
H.G. Hills Shopping Center
231 Franklin Road
Brentwood, Tennessee 37027
(615) 373-2741

▣ C & J Diner's Fried Chicken

1 (2-pound) frying chicken, cut
  up
2 cups all-purpose flour
1-1/2 teaspoons salt
1 teaspoon paprika
1 teaspoon pepper
1/4 teaspoon garlic powder
1/4 teaspoon onion powder
Vegetable oil

Combine all dry ingredients and roll chicken pieces in mixture. Heat oil to 350 degrees. Carefully lower chicken pieces into hot oil and fry for 20 to 25 minutes or until golden brown, turning once. Drain on paper towels and serve.

Serves 4

C & J DINER
137 Seventh Avenue North
Nashville, Tennessee 37203
(615) 255-6363

405 31st Avenue North
Nashville, Tennessee 37209
(615) 329-1120

Duck Cordon Bleu with Marinara Sauce

4 boneless, skinless duck breast
    halves, pounded to an even
    thinness
4 thin slices good-quality Swiss
    cheese
4 paper-thin slices prosciutto
Salt and pepper to taste
Granulated garlic to taste
1/4 teaspoon dried rosemary or
    thyme (optional)
5 eggs, beaten
1 cup all-purpose flour
Peanut oil

Cover each duck breast with a slice of cheese, then a slice of prosciutto. Roll into tight cylinders and place in the freezer until firm, but not frozen.

Preheat oven to 400 degrees. Add salt, pepper, and herbs (if desired) to the beaten eggs and set aside. Roll each duck breast cylinder in flour seasoned with salt, pepper, and granulated garlic, then dip each in egg mixture. Repeat process for all cylinders, dipping first in flour, then egg. Heat peanut oil to 400 degrees. Deep-fry duck in oil until light brown. Remove and drain on paper towels, then transfer to preheated oven for 10 to 15 minutes. To serve, slice duck and serve with **Marinara Sauce**.

Serves 4

Marinara Sauce

2 tablespoons extra-virgin olive
    oil
1 small onion, finely diced
2 cloves garlic, minced
1 tablespoon chopped fresh
    basil
1 tablespoon chopped fresh
    oregano
1/2 cup dry white wine
1/2 cup chicken stock
3 large tomatoes, peeled,
    seeded, and roughly
    chopped
Salt and white pepper to taste

Heat oil in a small stockpot over medium heat. Add onion, garlic, basil, and oregano. Reduce heat to low and cook until onion is translucent. Add wine and chicken stock, and reduce liquid by half. Stir in tomatoes and simmer over low heat for 15 minutes. Season with salt and white pepper.

Makes about 4 cups

ARTHUR'S IN UNION STATION
1001 Broadway
Nashville, Tennessee 37203
(615) 255-1494

Lamb Chops Dijonnaise with Red Pepper Jelly Sauce

16 lamb rib chops
Salt and pepper to taste
3 tablespoons hot Dijon
  mustard
4 tablespoons whole grain
  mustard
2 cups seasoned bread crumbs

Preheat oven to 400 degrees. Season lamb chops with salt and pepper. Combine mustards and spread lightly on lamb chops. Dredge in seasoned bread crumbs and bake for about 6 to 8 minutes (medium rare) or to desired doneness. Pour several spoonfuls of **Red Pepper Jelly Sauce** on each dinner plate, and serve lamb chops on top of the sauce.

This dish goes well with roasted potatoes and steamed asparagus.

Serves 4

Red Pepper Jelly Sauce

6 red bell peppers
1 jalapeño pepper
1 tablespoon cider vinegar
1/2 cup sugar
2 tablespoons cornstarch
1/4 cup water

Puree bell and jalapeño peppers, then add vinegar and sugar. Transfer to a saucepan and bring to a boil. Mix cornstarch with water and add to pepper mixture. Simmer until thickened.

Makes 2–3 cups

F. SCOTT'S
2220 Bandywood Drive
Nashville, Tennessee 37215
(615) 269-5861

☑ Grilled Rack of Lamb

2 (3-pound) racks of lamb
3 teaspoons ground rosemary
1 teaspoon pepper
1/2 teaspoon granulated garlic
1/2 teaspoon salt
1/4 cup A-1 Sauce
1/2 cup Worcestershire sauce

Prepare lamb by stripping away fatty covering and small bones. Cut away fat and meat between rib bones and scrape clean. (Lamb will now weigh approximately 1-1/4 pounds.) Split racks in half, allowing 4 or 5 ribs per serving. Cut slits vertically across loin about 1/2 inch deep between each rib bone. Combine rosemary, pepper, garlic, and salt. Sprinkle mixture generously on both sides of lamb. Combine A-1 and Worcestershire sauces. Grill lamb over medium heat for 15 to 20 minutes (medium well), basting generously from time to time with sauce. (*Note:* Rib bones may be wrapped in foil to prevent burning.)

Serves 4

OUR HOUSE
1059 Haley Road
Wartrace, Tennessee 37183
(800) 876-6616

☑ Veal Squirrel Hill

4 tablespoons clarified butter
  (see instructions on p. 26)
4 tablespoons diced shallots
8 (3-ounce) veal scallops,
  pounded and lightly dusted
  with flour
4 tablespoons finely diced red
  onion
1 cup wild mushrooms, sliced
1 cup roughly cut and
  stemmed fresh spinach
1 tablespoon all-purpose flour
1 cup Burgundy wine
1 cup beef stock

In a medium skillet, heat clarified butter. Add shallots and cook until tender (do not brown). Add veal and sauté until lightly browned on both sides. Add onion, mushrooms, and spinach. Stir in flour. Add wine and reduce mixture by half over low heat. Add beef stock and reduce mixture again by half. Place 2 veal scallops on each plate. Remove cooked vegetables from pan with a slotted spoon and arrange around veal. Pour sauce over veal and serve immediately.

Pair this delicious entree with a small loaf of French bread and glasses of Pinot Noir.

Serves 4

SUNSET GRILL
2001 Belcourt Avenue
Nashville, Tennessee 37212
(615) 386-3663

⦉Ⓩ⦊ Osso Buco with Risotto Milanese

2 veal shanks, cut into 3-inch
    pieces
All-purpose flour
1/4 cup butter
1 teaspoon salt
1/2 teaspoon pepper
1/2 cup finely chopped celery
1 medium onion, finely
    chopped
1/2 cup finely chopped carrots
1/2 cup minced mushrooms
1 large tomato, peeled, seeded,
    and chopped
1/2 teaspoon crumbled sage
1/2 teaspoon dried rosemary
2 cups dry white wine
Grated peel of 1 lemon
2 tablespoons chopped fresh
    parsley
1 clove garlic, minced

Coat veal shanks with flour. Heat butter in skillet and brown veal on all sides. Turn veal bones on their sides in skillet to retain marrow. Add salt, pepper, celery, onion, carrots, mushrooms, tomato, sage, and rosemary, and simmer, covered, for 10 minutes. Add wine and simmer, covered, for 2 hours. Combine lemon peel, parsley, and garlic, and stir in just before serving. Serve with **Risotto Milanese.**

Serves 6

Risotto Milanese

1 small onion, minced
1/2 cup (1 stick) butter
1-1/2 cups uncooked white rice
1 teaspoon saffron threads
4 cups chicken stock
2 tablespoons freshly grated
    Parmesan cheese

Sauté onion in 1/4 cup butter until lightly browned. Add rice and mix well. Soften saffron in 2 tablespoons of chicken stock. Add remaining stock to rice and bring to a boil. Simmer, covered, over low heat for 25 minutes, stirring frequently. Add remaining 1/4 cup butter and saffron. Simmer, uncovered, over low heat for 5 minutes more. Spoon onto a serving dish and sprinkle with Parmesan cheese.

Serves 6

MARIO'S
2005 Broadway
Nashville, Tennessee 37203
(615) 327-3232

☑ Jimmy Kelly's Chateaubriand

1 (2–3 pound) beef tenderloin
Freshly ground pepper
Seasoned salt
10–12 large white mushrooms,
  sliced
2-1/2 cups Cabernet Sauvignon
  or other dry red wine

Preheat oven to 450 degrees. Remove all fat from tenderloin and place flat on a large broiling pan. Coat beef with pepper and salt. Add mushrooms and 1 cup wine to broiling pan. Place in oven on middle rack and roast 10 minutes for rare, 20 additional minutes for well done. Remove tenderloin and mushrooms to a warm serving plate. Reserve wine in the pan.

Add remaining 1-1/2 cups wine to broiling pan. Deglaze pan by heating wine over high heat and stirring to loosen browned bits. Reduce mixture by half and season to taste. Slice tenderloin and serve with sauce on the side.

Excellent with fresh steamed cauliflower, asparagus, or broccoli.

Serves 4

JIMMY KELLY'S
217 Louise Avenue
Nashville, Tennessee 37203
(615) 329-4349

Black Jack Filet

4 (8-ounce) beef fillets
Juice of 2 oranges
5 cloves garlic, crushed
2 teaspoons grated fresh ginger
1/3 cup soy sauce
2 tablespoons firmly packed
   brown sugar
1 tablespoon toasted sesame
   seeds
1/3 cup Jack Daniel's whiskey

In a glass baking dish, combine orange juice, garlic, ginger, soy sauce, brown sugar, sesame seeds, and whiskey. Add beef and marinate overnight.

Remove beef and reserve marinade. Sear fillets in a skillet to preferred doneness and set aside. Add remaining marinade to the skillet and heat. Deglaze pan, stirring to loosen brown bits. Cook until sauce is reduced by half. Spoon sauce onto plates and top with steaks.

Excellent served with yam chips and a green vegetable. A country ham hollandaise, made by adding 1/4 cup thinly sliced and grilled country ham and 2 teaspoons chives to 1 cup of hollandaise sauce, is also good with this steak.

Serves 4

CROWN COURT
Regal Maxwell House Hotel
2025 MetroCenter Boulevard
Nashville, Tennessee 37228
(615) 259-4343

🔲 Never-Fail Roast Tenderloin

1 (3 to 3-1/2 pound) whole
   trimmed beef tenderloin
2 tablespoons dried basil
2 tablespoons coarsely ground
   pepper
1 tablespoon garlic salt
1/4 cup olive oil
Fresh basil leaves

Combine dried basil, pepper, garlic salt, and oil, and rub over meat. (*Note:* Can be prepared ahead to this point and refrigerated until ready to cook.) Transfer meat to a shallow roasting pan and roast in a preheated 400-degree oven, uncovered, exactly 30 minutes. (Meat will be rare.) Remove from oven, tent with foil, and allow to stand for 15 minutes to reabsorb juices. Slice and arrange on a serving platter, garnished with fresh basil.

Serve with tomato mayonnaise or horseradish sauce, **Clayton-Blackmon's Greek Salad***, and hard rolls.*

Serves 6 to 8 (dinner) or 20 (as an hors d'oeuvre on hard rolls)

**CLAYTON-BLACKMON GOURMET DELI AND
CATERING COMPANY**
4117 Hillsboro Road
Nashville, Tennessee 37215
(615) 297-3441

☑ Tenderloin with Green Peppercorns West End

6 (6-ounce) portions beef
  tenderloin
9 tablespoons unsalted butter
1/2 cup brandy
1/2 cup green peppercorns
1/2 cup heavy cream
Salt to taste

In a skillet, heat 3 tablespoons butter until medium brown. Sauté tenderloin in skillet to desired degree of doneness. Place on a large plate and keep warm.

Add brandy to skillet and deglaze pan over high heat, scraping bottom of pan to loosen drippings. Add peppercorns and boil down liquid until about 1/4 cup is left. Add cream. Whisk while adding remaining 6 tablespoons butter and bringing sauce to a boil. Season with salt to taste. Transfer sauce to a serving boat and serve immediately alongside tenderloin.

Serves 6

JULIAN'S RESTAURANT FRANÇAIS
formerly at
2412 West End Avenue
Nashville, Tennessee

🖭 Medallions of Beef Tenderloin with Scotch and Apples

8 (3-ounce) beef tenderloin
   medallions
3 tablespoons vegetable oil
Salt and pepper to taste
1 cup scotch whiskey
1/2 cup peeled and diced
   apples
2 cups beef stock or bouillon
1/2 teaspoon finely chopped
   cilantro
2 tablespoons butter
6 tablespoons maple syrup
Watercress sprigs

Heat oil in a skillet over medium-high heat. Season beef with salt and pepper and sauté on both sides to desired doneness. Pour off excess oil and discard. Deglaze pan with scotch, allowing liquid to reduce by half. Add diced apples and beef stock. Simmer for 1 to 2 minutes, then remove pan from heat. Stir in cilantro, butter, and maple syrup, and heat through. Top medallions with sauce and serve garnished with watercress.

Asparagus spears and red potatoes sautéed with garlic and rosemary go well with this dish.

Serves 4

THE STOCKYARD
901 Second Avenue North
Nashville, Tennessee 37201
(615) 255-6464

◪ Farmhouse Country-Fried Steak

2 pounds round steak
1/2 teaspoon salt
1/2 teaspoon pepper
1/2 cup all-purpose flour
1 tablespoon vegetable oil
1 onion, chopped
1 cup chicken stock or water
1 cup buttermilk
1 cup shredded cheddar
  cheese

Divide steak into serving portions. Pound each piece until thin, sprinkle with salt and pepper, and dust with flour. Heat oil in a skillet and sear meat until evenly brown on all sides. Add onions and cook for several minutes until limp. Combine chicken stock and buttermilk, and pour over meat. Stir to loosen bits of crust from bottom of skillet. Cover and cook over medium-low heat until meat is tender, about 45 to 50 minutes. (*Note:* Can be prepared ahead to this point.) Add cheese and stir into gravy.

This old-fashioned favorite is delicious over rice or biscuits.

Serves 6 to 8

MISS MARY BOBO'S BOARDING HOUSE
Main Street
Lynchburg, Tennessee 37352
(615) 759-7394

◪ Vanderbilt Meatloaf

2-1/2 pounds ground beef
1 generous cup diced green
   bell pepper
1 cup diced onion
3/4 cup diced celery
2 teaspoons freshly ground
   pepper
2 teaspoons salt
1 tablespoon Worcestershire
   sauce
2 eggs
1/4 cup plus 1 tablespoon milk
1-1/2 cups bread crumbs

Preheat oven to 250 degrees. Mix all ingredients except ground beef together. Combine mixture with ground beef and shape into a rectangle. Place in a baking pan with at least a 2-inch rim. Bake for 2 to 2-1/2 hours, or until firm to the touch.

Serve with mashed potatoes seasoned with chopped parsley, mustard greens, and diced green onions. Pipe or spoon mashed potatoes on top of meatloaf and dust with paprika. Brown quickly in a 475 degree oven or under a broiler.

Serves 10

ARNOLD'S COUNTRY KITCHEN
605 Eighth Avenue South
Nashville, Tennessee 37203
(615) 256-4455

ⓔ Boarding House Meatloaf

1-1/2 pounds ground beef
3/4 cup uncooked oatmeal
1-1/2 teaspoons salt
1/4 cup plus 2 tablespoons
  chopped green pepper
1/4 cup plus 2 tablespoons
  chopped onion
1 cup catsup
2 eggs
1/4 cup firmly packed brown
  sugar

Preheat oven to 350 degrees. Combine beef, oatmeal, salt, 1/4 cup bell pepper, 1/4 cup onion, 1/4 cup catsup, and eggs. Form mixture into a loaf. Place in a greased 9-by-3-inch loaf pan and bake for 1 hour. Pour off juice and bake for 10 minutes more.

In a saucepan, combine remaining 2 tablespoons bell pepper and onion, 3/4 cup catsup, and brown sugar. Simmer over low heat until onion and pepper are tender.

Transfer meatloaf to a platter, cover with sauce, and serve.

Serves 6 to 8

MISS MARY BOBO'S BOARDING HOUSE
Main Street
Lynchburg, Tennessee 37352
(615) 759-7394

▣ Home-Style Deep-Fried Spareribs

5 pounds pork spareribs
4 tablespoons soy sauce
2 tablespoons rice wine
1 tablespoon sugar
2 cups cornstarch
1 tablespoon salt
1 tablespoon MSG (optional)
1 teaspoon pepper
Vegetable oil

Cut spareribs into 2-inch long pieces. Combine soy sauce, wine, and sugar, and use to marinate spareribs for 30 minutes.

Combine cornstarch, salt, MSG, and pepper, and coat spareribs with mixture. Heat oil to 250 degrees and deep-fry spareribs for 3 minutes. Remove from oil. When ready to serve, reheat oil and deep-fry again over high heat for 20 seconds, until golden brown. Serve immediately.

Serves 4

DYNASTY RESTAURANT
3415 West End Avenue
Nashville, Tennessee 37203
(615) 269-0188

☑ Dragon Flower Pork

12 (1-ounce) medallions of
  pork loin, trimmed of excess
  fat
12 jumbo shrimp, peeled,
  deveined, and butterflied
4 tablespoons butter, melted
1 tablespoon plus 1 teaspoon
  minced garlic
Salt and pepper to taste
2 tablespoons sesame oil
1/4 cup chopped green onions
1/4 cup sherry
Juice and zest of 1 orange
1/2 cup Homemade Brown
  Sauce (see below)
2 dried Chinese hot peppers
Oriental rice noodles
  (cellophane or glass)

Using a metal skewer, thread shrimp and pork so that shrimp wraps around the circumference of the pork medallion. Place skewers on a baking sheet. Combine butter and 1 tablespoon garlic, and baste pork and shrimp with mixture. Season with salt and pepper. Roast under a hot broiler until shrimp and pork are firm (or cook over a charcoal grill).

Heat sesame oil in a saucepan over medium heat. Rapidly sauté green onions and remaining 1 teaspoon garlic, taking care not to brown them. Add sherry, orange juice and zest, **Homemade Brown Sauce**, and hot peppers to the pan, and simmer for 10 minutes. To serve, spoon sauce onto 4 dinner plates, slide pork and shrimp off skewers onto sauce, and garnish with rice noodles.

Serves 4

Homemade Brown Sauce

1 tablespoon butter
1 tablespoon flour
1/2 cup beef bouillon

In a small saucepan, melt butter and stir in flour. Simmer over medium heat for 5 minutes. Add beef bouillon and whisk gently for 5 minutes more until sauce thickens.

Makes 1/2 cup

BELLE MEADE BRASSERIE
101 Page Road
Nashville, Tennessee 37205
(615) 356-5450

⚡ Pork and Shrimp Khyber

1 (1-1/2) pound pork tenderloin, sliced into medallions
20–30 small shrimp, peeled and deveined
1/4 cup vegetable oil
1 green or red bell pepper, sliced
1 white onion, sliced
1 apple, peeled, cored, and diced
1/2 cup all-purpose flour
Salt and pepper to taste
1 tablespoon curry powder
1/2 cup mango chutney
3/4 cup pineapple juice
1 cup heavy cream
1 pound spinach fettuccine, cooked

Heat oil in skillet. Add bell pepper, onion, and apple, and sauté for 3 to 4 minutes. Lightly flour pork medallions, transfer medallions to pan, and season with salt and pepper. Toss with peppers, onion, and apples, and sauté mixture for 3 to 4 minutes more.

When pork is halfway done, add curry powder, chutney, and pineapple juice. Continue stirring so mixture doesn't stick to pan. Add cream. If mixture becomes too thick, add a little more pineapple juice or a dash of hot water. (*Note:* For a sweeter dish, add more chutney; for a spicier version, add a dash of cayenne or red pepper flakes.)

Lower heat, and add shrimp 5 minutes before serving. When shrimp are warm and cooked through, spoon mixture over warm spinach fettuccine and serve.

Serves 4 to 6

CAKEWALK RESTAURANT
3001 West End Avenue
Nashville, Tennessee 37203
(615) 320-7778

Sweet Endings

Jack Daniel's Ice Cream

7 large egg yolks
1/2 cup sugar
2 cups milk
1 cup heavy cream
1 vanilla bean, split
3/4 cup maple syrup
1/4 cup Jack Daniel's whiskey

Beat yolks with sugar until mixture becomes pale yellow. In a saucepan, heat milk, cream, and vanilla bean to a boil. Remove from heat and slowly whisk into egg yolks. Remove vanilla bean. Return mixture to medium heat and whisk constantly until slightly thickened. Remove from heat, then add maple syrup and whiskey. Refrigerate. When cold, transfer to an ice cream maker and freeze according to manufacturer's instructions.

Makes 1 quart

MISS MARY BOBO'S BOARDING HOUSE
Main Street
Lynchburg, Tennessee 37352
(615) 759-7394

Lemon Cooler Parfait

1 (8-ounce) container whipped
  topping (or whipped cream)
1 (14-ounce) can sweetened
  condensed milk
1 (6-ounce) can frozen
  lemonade concentrate
1 cup crushed graham crackers
1/4 cup sugar
1/2 cup (1 stick) butter, melted

Mix first 3 ingredients in a food processor or by hand until smooth. Set aside. Mix last 3 ingredients in a food processor. Alternately layer cream and crust mixtures in 4 parfait glasses and refrigerate until ready to serve.

Serves 4

THE SECOND STORY CAFE
Davis-Kidd Booksellers
4007 Hillsboro Road
Nashville, Tennessee 37215
(615) 385-0043

◼ Crème Brûlée

6 tablespoons dry brown sugar
(start with 1 cup firmly
packed brown sugar)
1 vanilla bean, split
2-1/4 cups heavy cream
6 egg yolks
12 tablespoons sugar
1-1/2–2 cups fresh raspberries

Dry the brown sugar by spreading 1 cup firmly packed brown sugar thinly on a baking sheet and placing it in a 350-degree oven for 1 minute. Allow sugar to cool at room temperature, then transfer it to a food processor and whirl until sugar looks like sand. Measure out 6 tablespoons and set aside.

Keep oven at 350 degrees. Combine split vanilla bean with cream and bring mixture to a boil. Remove from heat. Whip egg yolks and sugar together until lemon color. Slowly pour hot cream into egg mixture, stirring constantly. Skim off foam, strain, and pour into 6 individual oven-proof ramekins. Place in a large pan with enough hot water to come halfway up sides of ramekins. Bake in water bath until set, about 15 to 25 minutes. (*Note:* May be prepared to this point 2 to 3 days in advance.) Cool.

When ready to serve, spread 1 tablespoon of dry brown sugar in a thin layer over each of the 6 ramekins of cooled custard and brown under a broiler. (Brown sugar must be caramelized immediately before serving or it turns soft.) Serve with fresh raspberries.

Serves 6

F. SCOTT'S
2220 Bandywood Drive
Nashville, Tennessee 37215
(615) 269-5861

◼ Tiramisu

1 (4-ounce) package
   ladyfingers
1/4 cup espresso coffee
6 large eggs, separated
1/2 cup superfine sugar
1 pound ricotta cheese
3–4 ounces cream cheese,
   softened
1 tablespoon fresh lemon juice
1/2 cup heavy cream
2 tablespoons cocoa powder

Lay half the ladyfingers on a work surface and brush tops with half the coffee. Arrange in the bottom of a 9-by-13-inch pan. Beat egg yolks and sugar until light and fluffy. Blend ricotta, cream cheese, and lemon juice in a food processor until smooth. Add cheese mixture to egg yolks and sugar, and mix well. Beat egg whites until soft peaks form. Fold egg whites and heavy cream into cheese mixture. Spoon half the mixture over ladyfingers. Brush remaining ladyfingers with remaining coffee; arrange on top of creamy layer. Spread with remaining creamy mixture. Refrigerate, uncovered, for 2 hours. Just before serving, sprinkle with cocoa powder.

Serves 10 to 12

CAESAR'S RISTORANTE ITALIANO
Lion's Head Village
88 White Bridge Road
Nashville, Tennessee 37205
(615) 352-3661

◪ Chocolate Charlotte

2 (4-ounce) packages
   ladyfingers
3 cups heavy cream
1 (12-ounce) package chocolate
   chips
1/2 cup sugar
2/3 cup water
6 egg yolks
1/3 cup Grand Marnier
Additional whipped cream

Grease sides of an 8-inch springform pan with a little oil or shortening. Line sides with a strip of waxed paper. Cover bottom and sides with ladyfingers, then set aside.

Whip heavy cream until stiff and set aside.

Chop chocolate chips in a food processor. Combine sugar and water in a saucepan and bring to a boil. Pour boiling liquid into the food processor bowl containing the chocolate chips. Rapidly add egg yolks and Grand Marnier. Blend well. Gently fold chocolate mixture into reserved whipped cream and pour into ladyfinger-lined pan. Allow to set in the refrigerator for 3 to 4 hours or overnight.

To serve, open springform pan and remove waxed strip. Slice torte into portions, transfer to dessert plates, and garnish each slice with a dollop of whipped cream.

Serves 12

BELLE MEADE BRASSERIE
101 Page Road
Nashville, Tennessee 37205
(615) 356-5450

◼ Cold Lemon Soufflé

1-1/3 cups sugar
6 tablespoons all-purpose flour
4 eggs, separated
2 cups milk
Juice of 2 lemons
2 teaspoons grated lemon peel
1/2 teaspoon salt
8 thin lemon slices

Preheat oven to 350 degrees. Combine sugar and flour. Beat egg yolks well and add to milk. Combine with lemon juice, lemon peel, and salt. Beat egg whites until stiff and fold into lemon mixture.

Butter an 8-inch square baking dish. Pour in batter. Set into a larger pan of hot water and bake for 35 minutes. (*Note:* Can be made ahead and refrigerated when cooled.) When ready to serve, spoon onto dessert plates and garnish with a fresh lemon slice. Good served slightly warm or cooled.

This refreshing dessert also can be made in individual shallow ramekins. Shorten baking time by 10 minutes.

Serves 8

CHOICES RESTAURANT
108 Fourth Avenue South
Franklin, Tennessee 37064
(615) 791-0001

◼ Soufflé au Grand Marnier

1 cup whole milk
3 eggs, separated
1/4 cup flour
1/4 cup plus 2 tablespoons
   sugar
Grated peel of 1 orange
1/3 cup Grand Marnier
Powdered sugar

Place milk in a saucepan over medium heat. Mix egg yolks with flour, 1/4 cup sugar, and grated orange peel. When milk comes to a boil, remove from heat and stir in egg yolk mixture. Return to heat and bring to a boil again, whisking constantly. Simmer for 3 to 4 minutes, still stirring, until mixture has thickened. Remove from heat and stir in Grand Marnier. Cool.

Preheat oven to 400 degrees. Butter 4 individual soufflé dishes and dust with granulated sugar. Whip egg whites, adding remaining 2 tablespoons sugar while beating into soft peaks. Fold egg whites into cooled custard mixture. Divide between soufflé dishes and bake for 8 to 10 minutes until slightly brown on top. Remove and dust tops with powdered sugar.

Serves 4

JULIAN'S RESTAURANT FRANÇAIS
formerly at
2412 West End Avenue
Nashville, Tennessee

◼ New Orleans–Style Bread Pudding with Lemon Sauce

About 24 day-old croissants (enough for 20 cups), cut into 1-inch cubes
6 large eggs
2-1/2 cups sugar
1 tablespoon vanilla
1 tablespoon cinnamon
1/2 cup melted butter
1/4 cup brandy
1 quart milk
1 cup raisins
1 cup toasted pecans, walnuts, or almonds

Place bread cubes in a 9-by-13-inch glass baking dish. In a mixing bowl, combine eggs, sugar, vanilla, cinnamon, butter, and brandy. Blend well with a whisk. Add milk and blend together until smooth. Toss in raisins and nuts. Pour mixture over bread and allow to stand, refrigerated, for 1 hour or until all liquid is absorbed.

Preheat oven to 325 degrees. Bake bread pudding for 20 to 30 minutes until well browned and puffy. Pour **Lemon Sauce** over each serving.

Serves 12

Lemon Sauce

1/4 cup fresh lemon juice
1-1/2 cups cold water
1/2 cup sugar
4 teaspoons cornstarch
2 teaspoons vanilla

In a saucepan, bring lemon juice, 1 cup cold water, and sugar to a boil. Dissolve cornstarch in remaining 1/2 cup cold water, add vanilla, and pour into lemon mixture. Simmer until thickened.

Makes about 3 cups

THE SECOND STORY CAFE
Davis-Kidd Booksellers
4007 Hillsboro Road
Nashville, Tennessee 37215
(615) 385-0043

▣ Aunt Jessie's Whiskey Sour Bread Pudding

6 cups day-old white bread (or rolls) cubes
3 cups milk
3 eggs
1 cup sugar
1 tablespoon vanilla extract
1/2 teaspoon cinnamon
1/2 cup raisins
2 tablespoons butter or margarine

Place bread cubes in a bowl. Add milk and let stand for 5 minutes. Fold in eggs, sugar, vanilla, cinnamon, and raisins. Grease a 12-by-10-by-2-1/2-inch baking pan with butter or margarine. Transfer mixture to prepared pan and bake for 40 to 45 minutes until firm. (In a convection oven, lower temperature and baking time.) Serve with Whiskey Sour Sauce.

Serves 10

Whiskey Sour Sauce

Juice of 2 lemons
2 cups water
1 cup sugar
1/4 cup whiskey
1-1/2 tablespoons cornstarch
1 tablespoon water

Combine lemon juice with water and sugar. Cook over medium heat until slightly syrupy. Stir in whiskey. Combine cornstarch and water, add to sauce, and cook until thickened.

Makes about 3-1/2 cups

ARNOLD'S COUNTRY KITCHEN
605 Eighth Avenue South
Nashville, Tennessee 37203
(615) 256-4455

◩ Shadowbrook's Pecan Pie

3 large eggs
1 cup firmly packed light
  brown sugar
1 cup light corn syrup
1/4 cup melted butter
1/2 teaspoon salt
1 teaspoon vanilla extract
2 tablespoons peach schnapps,
  plus additional to garnish
1 cup chopped pecans
2 unbaked 8- or 9-inch pie
  shells
Whipped cream
Strawberry, kiwi, and peach
  slices

Preheat oven to 400 degrees. Beat eggs, then add brown sugar and corn syrup. Mix together. Add butter, salt, vanilla, and peach schnapps. Mix well. Add pecans and beat again. Pour into unbaked pie shells and bake for 10 minutes. Reduce oven temperature to 350 degrees and continue baking for 30 minutes more. To serve, decorate each portion with whipped cream and slices of strawberry, kiwi, and peach. If desired, top each serving with a teaspoon of peach schnapps. (*Note:* This pie freezes well).

Serves 8 to 12

SHADOWBROOK
5397 Rawlings Road
Joelton, Tennessee 37080
(615) 876-0700

◪ Tropical Silk Pie

1 (9-inch) pie shell, pricked
   and baked until golden
   brown
1 cup (2 sticks) butter, cut into
   1/2-inch cubes
2 cups sugar
4 ounces unsweetened
   chocolate, melted and
   cooled
2 teaspoons vanilla extract
4 eggs
3 tablespoons rum

Cream butter and sugar in a food processor. Add chocolate and vanilla and set on high speed for 10 minutes. Add eggs one at a time, mixing well after each addition. Add rum and continue mixing until smooth and silky (mixture should not be granular). Immediately pour into baked and cooled pie shell. Smooth top with a spatula and refrigerate for 4 hours.

Rum gives this pie its tropical, coconut-like flavor.

Serves 6

RAINBOW KEY
Lion's Head Village
80 White Bridge Road
Nashville, Tennessee 37205
(615) 352-7252

◼ Black Bottom Pie

1 (9-inch) pie crust, baked
1 cup sugar
2 tablespoons cornstarch
1 (1-ounce) square chocolate
2 dashes of salt
1/2 cup water
1-1/2 tablespoons butter
1 teaspoon vanilla
1 tablespoon gelatin
1/4 cup cold milk
1-1/3 cups hot scalded milk
2 egg yolks, slightly beaten
2 egg whites, stiffly beaten
1 cup heavy cream, whipped
Grated unsweetened chocolate

Combine 1/2 cup sugar, cornstarch, chocolate, dash of salt, water, and butter in a saucepan. Cook, stirring constantly, until mixture thickens. Continue to cook for 2 minutes more, then stir in 1/2 teaspoon vanilla. Remove from heat and set aside.

Place gelatin in cold milk and let stand for at least 3 minutes. Mix with hot scalded milk. Beat egg yolks slightly with remaining 1/2 cup sugar and a dash of salt. Pour hot milk mixture over yolks, stirring constantly. Transfer to a double boiler and cook until mixture coats a spoon. Continue to stir constantly. Remove from heat and add remaining 1/2 teaspoon vanilla. Cool, stirring until slightly thickened. Mixture should be firm before folding in stiffly beaten egg whites.

To assemble pie, layer reserved chocolate mixture over bottom and up sides of crust. Top with custard. Refrigerate for several hours until set. When ready to serve, top with whipped cream and sprinkle with grated chocolate.

Serves 6 to 8

SATSUMA TEA ROOM
417 Union Street
Nashville, Tennessee 37219
(615) 256-0760

❂ Heavenly Chocolate Pie

1 (9-inch) pie shell, baked
2 eggs, separated
1/2 teaspoon vinegar
1/4 teaspoon plus 1/8 teaspoon
 cinnamon
3/4 cup sugar
1/4 teaspoon salt
1 cup semisweet chocolate
 morsels
1/4 cup water
1 cup heavy cream

Beat together egg whites, vinegar, 1/4 teaspoon cinnamon, and 1/2 cup sugar until stiff. Spread mixture over bottom and up sides of baked pie shell. Bake in a preheated 325-degree oven for 18 to 20 minutes or until meringue is lightly browned. While meringue bakes, mix together chocolate morsels and water. Microwave on high until chocolate melts. Immediately beat in egg yolks using a wire whisk. Blend well and cool. Spread half of chocolate mixture over cooled meringue. Put half-filled pie and remaining chocolate mixture in refrigerator to chill.

When both have chilled, beat heavy cream until stiff, adding remaining amounts of cinnamon and sugar. Layer half of the whipped cream mixture over chilled chocolate layer.

For the final layer, combine remaining chocolate mixture and remaining whipped cream mixture and spread in center of pie. Chill all day before serving. (*Note:* Can be made 2 days ahead.)

Serves 8

THE PUFFY MUFFIN
H.G. Hills Shopping Center
231 Franklin Road
Brentwood, Tennessee 37027
(615) 373-2741

▣ Chocolate Chip Pecan Pie

1/4 cup (1/2 stick) butter or
    margarine
3 eggs
3/4 cup sugar
3/4 cup light corn syrup
1/4 cup chocolate chips, plus
    extra to garnish
1/2 cup pecan pieces
1 (9-inch) pie shell, unbaked
Whipped cream

Preheat oven to 350 degrees. Melt butter or margarine and set aside. Mix eggs and sugar. Add syrup and melted butter. Spread chocolate chips and pecan pieces over bottom of pie shell. Pour egg and sugar mixture over chocolate and pecans. Bake for about 35 minutes. (*Note:* Can be made 1 day ahead, and freezes well.)

Serves 8

THE PINEAPPLE ROOM
Cheekwood
1200 Forest Park Drive
Nashville, Tennessee 37205
(615) 352-4859

◙ Norwegian Apple Pie with Rum Sauce

1 egg
1 cup all-purpose flour
1 cup sugar
1 cup applesauce
1 teaspoon cinnamon
1 teaspoon nutmeg
1 teaspoon baking soda
1 teaspoon salt
3/4 cup pecan pieces
1/2 cup (1 stick) butter, melted

Preheat oven to 350 degrees. Combine all ingredients and pour into a buttered 10-inch pie pan. Bake until center springs back from gentle pressure, about 45 minutes. Pour **Rum Sauce** over pie as soon as it comes out of the oven. Allow sauce to soak in.

Serve with whipped cream or ice cream.

Serves 8

Rum Sauce

3 tablespoons rum
1/4 cup firmly packed brown
  sugar
1/4 cup heavy cream

Combine all ingredients in a saucepan and warm just until sugar dissolves.

Makes about 1/2 cup

THE PINEAPPLE ROOM
Cheekwood
1200 Forest Park Drive
Nashville, Tennessee 37205
(615) 352-4859

Hot Apple Tart Patrice

1 sheet frozen puff pastry
3 Granny Smith apples
2/3 cup unsalted butter
2/3 cup sugar

Preheat oven to 350 degrees. Cut puff pastry into 6 circles, 3 inches in diameter, and place on a greased baking sheet.

Peel and core apples, then slice them thinly. Divide apple slices among pastry circles, arranging them attractively. Top each tart with an equal portion of butter and sprinkle with sugar. Bake for 15 to 20 minutes.

Serve with ice cream, sherbet, or a fruit sauce.

Serves 6

JULIAN'S RESTAURANT FRANÇAIS
formerly at
2412 West End Avenue
Nashville, Tennessee

❖ Chocolate Chess Pecan Pie

1/4 cup (1/2 stick) butter
3 tablespoons cocoa powder
1-1/2 cups sugar
2 eggs
3/4 cup evaporated milk
3/4 cup pecans
1 (9-inch) pie shell, unbaked
Whipped cream (optional)

Melt butter and stir in cocoa. Add sugar and mix well. Add eggs, one at a time. Gradually stir in evaporated milk, followed by pecans. (*Note:* Can be prepared ahead to this point and refrigerated for several days; stir before pouring into pie shell.) Pour filling into unbaked pie shell and bake at 325 degrees for 40 to 45 minutes. (Pie will "poof" over crust when done, but will settle when removed from oven.) Serve with a dollop of whipped cream, if desired.

This pie freezes and travels well, which makes it a natural for housewarmings and potluck dinners.

Serves 6

11/27/97

20 min for individual tarts

MERRIDEE'S BREAD BASKET
110 Fourth Avenue South
Franklin, Tennessee 37604
(615) 790-3755

◧ Brandy Alexander Pie

1 (1-pound) box chocolate
   wafers
2 tablespoons butter, melted
1 cup plus 1 tablespoon sugar
3/4 cup heavy cream
2 large egg yolks (or egg
   substitutes)
1 teaspoon plain gelatin
2 tablespoons cold water
1/2 teaspoon vanilla flavoring
Dash of nutmeg
1/4 cup brandy
Fresh strawberries

In a food processor or blender, process cookies into fine crumbs. Reserve 1 tablespoon for garnish. Combine remaining crumbs with butter and 1 tablespoon sugar. Transfer mixture into a 9-inch pie pan. With a small spatula, press crumb mixture evenly along bottom and up sides of pan. Use an empty pie tin to press crumbs firmly into a crust. Set aside.

In a bowl, whip cream until stiff. Set aside. In another bowl, whip egg yolks until light, then gradually beat in remaining 1/2 cup sugar. Soften gelatin in cold water, then heat slowly in a double boiler over low heat until gelatin has dissolved. With mixer on low speed, add gelatin, vanilla, nutmeg, and brandy to egg yolk mixture. Gently fold in whipped cream with a whisk. Pour mixture into prepared pie shell. Sprinkle reserved crumbs through a strainer over pie and allow to set for 30 minutes. Cover and place in freezer to chill and firm. (*Note:* Can be made several days ahead, and keeps in freezer for up to 1 month.)

When ready to serve, halve strawberries and place around the rim of the pie.

Serves 8

SPERRY'S
5109 Harding Road
Nashville, Tennessee 37205
(615) 353-0809

◉ Our House Italian Cream Cake

5 eggs, separated
1/2 cup (1 stick) butter, room
  temperature
1 cup shortening
2 cups sugar
2 cups all-purpose flour
1 teaspoon baking soda
1 cup buttermilk
1 teaspoon vanilla extract
1/2 cup chopped pecans
1 cup sweetened flaked
  coconut

Preheat oven to 350 degrees. Beat egg whites until stiff, then set aside. In a large bowl, cream butter, shortening, and sugar. Add egg yolks, beating to incorporate. Sift flour and soda together, then add to yolk mixture alternately with buttermilk. Stir in vanilla, nuts, and coconut. Fold in beaten egg whites. Pour mixture into 3 greased and floured 9-inch cake pans and bake for 30 to 35 minutes. Turn onto wire racks and cool completely before frosting.

Spread **Italian Cream Frosting** between layers and on top and sides of cake. Refrigerate for 3 hours before serving.

Serves 16

Italian Cream Frosting

3 (3-ounce) packages cream
  cheese, softened
6 tablespoons butter, softened
1-1/2 pounds powdered sugar
1 teaspoon vanilla extract
1/2 cup chopped pecans

Cream together cheese and butter. Gradually beat in sugar and vanilla, then stir in nuts.

Makes about 6 cups

OUR HOUSE
1059 Haley Road
Wartrace, Tennessee 37183
(800) 876-6616

▨ Schuss à la Val D'Isére

2 eggs plus 2 egg yolks
1-3/4 cups plus 2 tablespoons
 sugar
1/4 cup sifted all-purpose flour
1 cup water
2 cups heavy cream
1 ounce (2 tablespoons) gelatin
1 cup sour cream
Seasonal red fruits

Preheat oven to 400 degrees. To make cake, beat 2 eggs and 1/4 cup sugar in a bowl over a pan of simmering water until warm. Remove from over water and beat until thickened and cool. Fold sifted flour into egg mixture and pour into a 6-inch greased and floured cake pan. Bake for 30 minutes. Remove cake from pan and, when cool, cut into 2 cake layers.

Make sugar syrup by bringing 1/2 cup water and 1/2 cup sugar to a boil over low heat. Stir until sugar dissolves, then increase heat and boil for 1 minute. Set aside.

To make filling, in a bowl over simmering water, sprinkle 1 cup sugar over 2 egg yolks, whisking briskly. Remove from heat and let cool. Dissolve gelatin in 1/2 cup water and add when egg yolks are almost cold. Mix until mixture is smooth, then fold in sour cream.

To assemble, place 1 cake layer back in the cake pan. Using a pastry bush, moisten cake with half the sugar syrup. Top with filling. Cover with second cake layer and moisten with remaining sugar syrup. Refrigerate.

When cake has set, whip heavy cream to soft peaks, adding 2 tablespoons sugar. Place a cardboard disk or plate on top of cake in pan and turn cake out onto a serving plate. Mask cake completely with whipped cream, reserving some for garnish. Decorate top of cake attractively with red fruit, then, with a pastry bag fitted with a plain nozzle tip, pipe swirls of whipped cream around the cake.

Serves 8

RHETT'S
Opryland Hotel
2800 Opryland Drive
Nashville, Tennessee 37214
(615) 889-1000

◪ Poppy Seed Bread with Orange Glaze

3 cups all-purpose flour
2-1/2 cups sugar
1-1/2 teaspoons baking powder
1-1/2 teaspoons salt
1-1/2 tablespoons poppy seeds
3 eggs
1-1/2 cups milk
1-1/8 cups oil
1-1/2 teaspoons vanilla extract
1-1/2 teaspoons almond extract
1-1/2 teaspoons butter
  flavoring

Preheat oven to 350 degrees. Stir together flour, sugar, baking powder, salt, and poppy seeds. Set aside. Mix together eggs, milk, oil, and flavorings. Combine wet and dry mixtures until well blended. Spray 2 regular-sized loaf pans or 4 small loaf pans with nonstick vegetable spray. Pour batter into pans. Bake for 1 hour for regular size, and about 45 minutes for small size. Bread will be done when batter leaves sides of pan.

After removing bread from oven, poke holes in loaves with a toothpick or a cake tester and pour **Orange Glaze** over warm bread. Keeps well for several days.

Serve 16

Orange Glaze

1/4 cup orange juice
3/4 cup sugar
1/2 teaspoon vanilla extract
1/2 teaspoon almond extract
1/2 teaspoon butter flavoring

Combine ingredients and mix well until sugar is dissolved (may be heated gently to dissolve sugar).

Makes about 3/4 cup

BIDDLE'S LUNCH BOX
Koger Center, Gatlinburg Building
7101 Executive Center Drive
Brentwood, Tennessee 37027
(615) 370-8565

◪ Lemon Bread

3/4 cup (1-1/2 sticks) butter
1-1/2 cups sugar
3 eggs
2-1/4 cups all-purpose flour
1/4 teaspoon salt
1/4 teaspoon baking soda
3/4 cup buttermilk
Grated zest of 1 lemon
Juice of 2 lemons
3/4 cup powdered sugar

Preheat oven to 325 degrees. Cream butter until smooth. Add sugar and eggs, and mix well. Beat in dry ingredients alternately with buttermilk. Fold in lemon zest. Pour batter into 2 small loaf pans sprayed with nonstick vegetable spray. Bake for 1 hour, or until bread pulls away from pan.

Make glaze by combining lemon juice and powdered sugar until sugar dissolves. After removing bread from oven, poke holes in loaf with a toothpick and pour glaze over warm bread. (*Note:* Keeps well for several days.)

Serves 16

BIDDLE'S LUNCH BOX
Koger Center, Gatlinburg Building
7101 Executive Center Drive
Brentwood, Tennessee 37027
(615) 370-8565

◾ Hummingbird Cake with Cream Cheese Frosting

1/4 teaspoon ground cloves
3 cups all-purpose flour
2 cups sugar
1 teaspoon baking soda
1 teaspoon salt
2 teaspoons ground cinnamon
3 eggs, beaten
1 cup vegetable oil
1 tablespoon vanilla extract
1 (8-ounce) can crushed
    pineapple, undrained
2 cups chopped pecans
2-1/2 cups chopped bananas

Preheat oven to 350 degrees. In a large bowl, combine first 6 ingredients, then add eggs and oil. Stir together until dry ingredients are moistened. Do not beat. Stir in vanilla, pineapple, 1 cup pecans, and bananas. Spoon batter into 3 greased and floured 9-inch cake pans. Bake for 25 to 30 minutes. Cool in pans for 10 minutes, then remove cake layers. Cool completely, then frost between cake layers and on top and sides of cake with **Cream Cheese Frosting**. Pat remaining chopped pecans over top and sides of cake.

Serves 10 to 12

Cream Cheese Frosting

1 (8-ounce) package cream
    cheese, softened
1/2 cup (1 stick) butter,
    softened
1 (1-pound) box powdered
    sugar, sifted
1 teaspoon vanilla extract

Combine cream cheese and butter, and beat until smooth. Add powdered sugar and vanilla, beating until mixture is light and fluffy.

Makes about 3-1/2 cups

MOSKO'S MUNCHEONETTE
2204 Elliston Place
Nashville, Tennessee 37203
(615) 327-2658

▦ Caramel Pound Cake with Caramel Frosting

1-1/2 cups (3 sticks) butter
1 (1-pound) box dark brown
  sugar
1 cup sugar
5 large eggs
3 cups all-purpose flour, sifted
1/2 teaspoon baking powder
1 cup milk
2 teaspoons vanilla extract

Preheat oven to 325 degrees. Cream butter until fluffy. Add sugars and mix well. Add eggs one at a time, beating after each addition. Sift together flour and baking powder, and add alternately to batter with milk and vanilla, beginning and ending with flour mixture. Pour into a regular-sized loaf pan sprayed with nonstick vegetable spray. Bake for 1-1/2 hours, or until a knife inserted into the center comes out clean. Remove from oven and allow to stand about 10 minutes before removing from pan. Ice with **Caramel Frosting**. (*Note:* Keeps well for several days.)

Serves 8

Caramel Frosting

1 cup firmly packed light
  brown sugar
1/4 cup (1/2 stick) butter
1/3 cup milk
2 cups powdered sugar
1 teaspoon vanilla extract

Combine brown sugar, butter, and milk in a heavy saucepan, and bring to a boil over low heat. Simmer for 5 minutes, stirring constantly. Cool. Using an electric mixer, gradually beat in powdered sugar and vanilla until a spreading consistency is achieved.

Makes about 3 cups

THE PUFFY MUFFIN
H.G. Hills Shopping Center
231 Franklin Road
Brentwood, Tennessee 37027
(615) 373-2741

Chocolate Sheet Cake with Chocolate Nut Frosting

2 cups sugar
2 cups flour
1/2 teaspoon salt
1 cup (2 sticks) butter or
   margarine
4 tablespoons cocoa powder
1 cup water
2 eggs, well beaten
1/2 cup buttermilk
1 teaspoon baking soda
1 teaspoon vanilla extract

Preheat oven to 350 degrees. Sift together sugar, flour, and salt. Melt butter, cocoa, and water over medium heat just to boiling. Pour over flour mixture and stir well. Add eggs, buttermilk, baking soda, and vanilla, and stir together until well blended. Pour into a well-greased 9-by-13-inch baking pan and bake for 30 to 35 minutes. Ice with Chocolate Nut Frosting while cake is still warm.

Serves 15 to 20

This standard favorite can be adapted to "fancier" presentations, such as Bundt or springform pans, by cooking about 5 minutes longer. Drizzle the frosting in these cases instead of spreading it.

Chocolate Nut Frosting

1/2 cup (1 stick) butter or
   margarine
4 tablespoons cocoa powder
6 tablespoons milk
1 teaspoon vanilla extract
1 (1-pound) box powdered
   sugar
1 cup chopped nuts

Melt butter with cocoa over low heat. Add milk, vanilla, powdered sugar, and nuts, and stir well.

Makes about 3 cups

ROTIER'S RESTAURANT
2413 Elliston Place
Nashville, Tennessee 37203
(615) 327-9892

Jack Daniel's Chocolate Birthday Cake

1-1/2 cups water
1/2 cup plus 2 tablespoons Jack
  Daniel's whiskey
1 tablespoon instant coffee
  granules
1-1/4 cups (2-1/2 sticks) butter
1 cup cocoa powder
2 cups sugar
2 eggs
2 cups all-purpose flour
2 teaspoons baking powder
1/8 teaspoon salt
1 cup chopped pecans

Preheat oven to 325 degrees. In a very large saucepan, heat water, 1/2 cup whiskey, coffee, butter, and cocoa until butter melts. Remove from heat. Beat in sugar, then eggs. In a bowl, stir together flour, baking powder, and salt. Beat into chocolate mixture until incorporated. Stir in pecans. Turn batter into a greased and floured tube pan. Bake for about 1 hour, or until a tester inserted in the center comes out clean. Immediately sprinkle with the remaining 2 tablespoons whiskey. Cool in pan on a wire rack, then remove cake from pan.

Try topped with a chocolate glaze or powdered sugar and served alongside fresh berries.

Serves 8

MISS MARY BOBO'S BOARDING HOUSE
Main Street
Lynchburg, Tennessee 37352
(615) 759-7394

❋ Amaretto Mascarpone Cheesecake

2 cups graham cracker crumbs
1-1/2 cups sugar
1/4 cup all-purpose flour
6 tablespoons melted butter
1-1/2 pounds mascarpone
   cheese
4 eggs
1 cup amaretto
2 tablespoons cornstarch
3 cups sour cream
1 teaspoon almond extract
Toasted almonds
Whipped cream

Preheat oven to 350 degrees. In a stainless steel bowl, combine graham cracker crumbs, 1/2 cup sugar, 2 tablespoons flour, and melted butter. Spread mixture evenly over the bottom of a 9-inch springform pan and pack firmly.

Soften mascarpone cheese in a food processor bowl. Blend in eggs and 1 cup sugar. Pulse processor a few times to combine thoroughly. Blend in amaretto, cornstarch, 2 tablespoons flour, sour cream, and almond extract. Process until mixture is smooth and then pour into prepared pan. Place pan on a baking sheet and bake for 1 hour. Cake is done when center is set. Remove from oven and cool to room temperature. Refrigerate overnight.

Remove sides of pan, slice, and serve garnished with toasted almonds and whipped cream.

Serves 16

FINEZZA
5404 Harding Road
Nashville, Tennessee 37205
(615) 356-9398

❀ Banana Split Cheesecake

3 cups vanilla wafers, crushed
1-1/2 cups roasted peanuts,
   plus additional to garnish
1-1/4 cups sugar
8 teaspoons softened butter
2 (8-ounce) packages cream
   cheese, softened
2 teaspoons fresh lemon juice
4 eggs
3/4 cup sour cream
4 medium-to-large very ripe
   bananas, mashed
Whipped cream
Peanuts
Chocolate sauce
Maraschino cherries

Preheat oven to 350 degrees. In a food processor, combine vanilla wafers, peanuts, 1/2 cup sugar, and butter. Pat crust mixture into bottom and three-fourths up sides of a 10-inch springform pan. Line outside of pan with foil, shiny side facing out.

Process together cream cheese, 3/4 cup sugar, lemon juice, eggs, sour cream, and bananas until smooth. Pour mixture into prepared pan and bake for 1 hour, or until cheesecake is light brown on top. Cool completely at room temperature and then chill for at least 12 hours before serving.

Garnish individual servings with a dollop of whipped cream, chopped peanuts, a drizzle of chocolate sauce, and a maraschino cherry on top.

Serves 12

FAISON'S
2000 Belcourt Avenue
Nashville, Tennessee 37212
(615) 298-2112

◙ Sour Mash Cheesecake

1-1/2 cups finely crushed Oreo
   cookies
2 tablespoons melted butter
3 (8-ounce) packages cream
   cheese, softened
1 (14-ounce) can condensed
   milk
3 eggs
2 teaspoons vanilla extract
1 teaspoon cinnamon
3/4 cup sour mash whiskey
1 cup sour cream
2 ounces semisweet chocolate
1/4 cup heavy cream

Preheat oven to 350 degrees. Combine cookie crumbs and butter, then press firmly onto the bottom of a 9-inch springform pan.

Beat cream cheese until soft, gradually adding milk, eggs, vanilla, cinnamon, and whiskey. Beat until smooth. Pour into prepared pan and bake for 1 hour, or until center is springy. Loosen cake from side of pan and allow to cool. Spread with sour cream.

In a saucepan, combine chocolate and heavy cream. Stir over low heat until melted together and smooth. Drizzle chocolate glaze over each serving of cake.

Serves 8 to 10

THE WILD BOAR
2014 Broadway
Nashville, Tennessee 37203
(615) 329-1313

❖ Jubilee Chocolate Cheesecake

2 cups chocolate wafer crumbs
6 tablespoons butter, melted
3 tablespoons sugar
3 (8-ounce) packages cream
  cheese, softened
1 cup plus 2 tablespoons firmly
  packed light brown sugar
3 tablespoons Jack Daniel's
  whiskey
2 (1-ounce) semisweet
  chocolate squares, melted
3 eggs
Shaved chocolate squares

Preheat oven to 325 degrees. Combine first 3 ingredients, mix well, and press firmly into an 8- or 9-inch springform pan. Bake for 10 minutes, then allow to cool.

Combine cream cheese, brown sugar, and whiskey. Mix until well blended. Add melted chocolate and eggs, one at a time, beating well after each addition. Pour mixture into prepared pan and bake for 35 to 40 minutes. Cool, then chill. Garnish with shaved chocolate squares and serve. (*Note:* Can be made several days ahead.)

Serves 18 to 24

MISS MARY BOBO'S BOARDING HOUSE
Main Street
Lynchburg, Tennessee 37352
(615) 759-7394

❀ Chocolate Almond Truffles

10 ounces bittersweet
    chocolate, grated
6 tablespoons unsalted butter
1/2 cup heavy cream
1 tablespoon brandy (optional)
1 pound couverture chocolate,
    for coating (found in
    gourmet stores)
2 cups sliced almonds, toasted

In a double boiler over medium heat, place grated chocolate, butter, and heavy cream. Stir ingredients until melted. Add brandy and pour into a shallow pan. Refrigerate until mixture is firm.

Scoop mixture into walnut-sized (about 1 tablespoon) balls and place on a waxed paper–covered tray. Melt couverture chocolate over very low heat (or chocolate will burn), stirring frequently. Continue to stir until chocolate cools down to 85 degrees (slightly cooler than the back of your finger). Using a fork, dip balls into melted couverture chocolate. Roll each in toasted almonds. (*Note:* Filling can be made weeks in advance and frozen. Covered truffles will keep refrigerated for 1 month in an airtight container.)

Serve these confections with coffee, tea, or brandy.

Makes 30 to 36

MERE BULLES
152 Second Avenue North
Nashville, Tennessee 37201
(615) 256-1946

▨ Espresso Hazelnut Brownies

6 ounces unsweetened
   chocolate
3/4 cup (1-1/2 sticks) unsalted
   butter
1 tablespoon instant espresso
   powder
4 eggs, room temperature
2 cups sugar
1 teaspoon vanilla extract
1 cup flour
1-2/3 cups chopped hazelnuts

Preheat oven to 350 degrees. Melt chocolate, butter, and espresso powder together in a double boiler, then cool. Beat eggs and sugar together, then add to cooled chocolate mixture. Blend well, then stir in remaining ingredients (do not overmix). Pour into a greased and floured 8-by-14-inch pan and bake for 25 minutes. Cool, then spread with **Espresso Hazelnut Icing**. (*Note:* Brownies freeze well before they are iced).

Serves 8 to 10

Espresso Hazelnut Icing

6 tablespoons butter
3 ounces bittersweet chocolate
1 cup firmly packed brown
   sugar
3/4 cup heavy cream

Melt butter and chocolate in a heavy saucepan, stirring constantly. Add brown sugar and cream. Bring to a boil and cook for 3 minutes or until thick enough to spread. Cool slightly and spread on brownies; icing will gradually harden.

Makes 1-1/2 cups

THE CORNER MARKET
Westgate Shopping Center
6051 Highway 100
Nashville, Tennessee 37205
(615) 352-6772

▣ Lemon Squares

1/2 cup (1 stick) unsalted
  butter, melted
1/8 teaspoon salt
1 cup all-purpose flour
1/4 cup powdered sugar, plus
  additional to garnish
1/2 teaspoon baking powder
1 cup sugar
2 eggs, beaten
2 tablespoons fresh lemon
  juice
Grated lemon zest

Preheat oven to 325 degrees. In a bowl, combine melted butter, salt, flour, and powdered sugar. Pat mixture into a 7-by-11-inch baking dish to form a crust. Bake for 15 to 20 minutes, then cool.

Increase oven temperature to 350 degrees. Combine remaining ingredients and spread over baked crust. Bake for an additional 20 to 25 minutes. When cool, cut into squares and remove from pan. Sprinkle with powdered sugar and lemon zest. (*Note:* To freeze, layer squares with waxed paper in an airtight container.)

These scrumptious bites go well with vanilla ice cream.

Makes 36 squares

THE PICNIC, INC.
4334 Harding Road
Nashville, Tennessee 37205
(615) 297-5398

▣ Tennessee Berry Crisp

3/4 cup quick-cooking rolled
   oats
3/4 cup firmly packed brown
   sugar
1/4 cup all-purpose flour
1/4 teaspoon salt
1/4 cup (1/2 stick) butter or
   margarine
1 quart fresh blackberries or
   raspberries, washed and
   hulled
2 tablespoons sugar

Preheat oven to 350 degrees. In a medium bowl, combine oats, brown sugar, flour, and salt. Cut in butter until mixture resembles coarse crumbs. Set aside.

Place berries in a 10-by-6-by-2-inch baking dish. Sprinkle first with sugar, then with crumb mixture. Bake for 40 to 45 minutes, then serve warm.

Offer these with fresh heavy cream or ice cream.

Serves 6

MISS MARY BOBO'S BOARDING HOUSE
Main Street
Lynchburg, Tennessee 37352
(615) 759-7394

◼ Molasses Sugar Cookies

3/4 cup shortening (half butter)
1 cup sugar plus extra for
  rolling
1/4 cup molasses or sorghum
1 egg
2 teaspoons soda
1/2 teaspoon ground cloves
2 cups all-purpose flour
1/2 teaspoon ground ginger
1 teaspoon ground cinnamon
1/2 teaspoon salt

In a 3- or 4-quart saucepan, melt shortening, then let cool. Add sugar, molasses, and egg, and beat well. Sift together dry ingredients and add, all at once, to first mixture. Mix until well blended. Chill batter for at least 1 hour.

Preheat oven to 375 degrees. Form dough into 1-inch balls, roll in sugar, and place on a baking sheet 1 inch apart. Bake for 8 to 10 minutes, just until cookies are set and lightly browned. Cookies should have a crunchy exterior and chewy interior when cool. (*Note:* Dough can be frozen after forming into balls; thaw completely before rolling in sugar.)

Makes 24

MERRIDEE'S BREAD BASKET
110 Fourth Avenue South
Franklin, Tennessee 37604
(615) 790-3755

◉ Tutti Frutti Flambé

3 whole fresh pineapples
3 peeled navel oranges, white
   membrane removed
1 cup seedless grapes
Cherries, plums, peaches, or
   ripe cantaloupe, chunked
1/3 cup bourbon whiskey
2 tablespoons orange extract
4 tablespoons sugar
6 small scoops French vanilla
   ice cream
1 cup sweetened whipped
   cream

Split pineapples lengthwise, leaving green tops on. Cut out flesh in long strips, and discard core. Arrange strips in pineapple shells with other fresh fruits and sprinkle with bourbon. (*Note:* Can be prepared to this point and refrigerated for several hours.)

Shortly before serving, mix orange extract with sugar. When ready to serve, place a scoop of ice cream in the center of each filled pineapple shell. Dab with sweetened whipped cream and saturated orange sugar. Using a match, carefully light the orange sugar and serve immediately.

If flaming is not desired, serve these fruit boats with a cherry on top.

Serves 6

HACHLAND HILL INN
1601 Madison Street
Clarksville, Tennessee 37043
(615) 647-1400

Restaurants

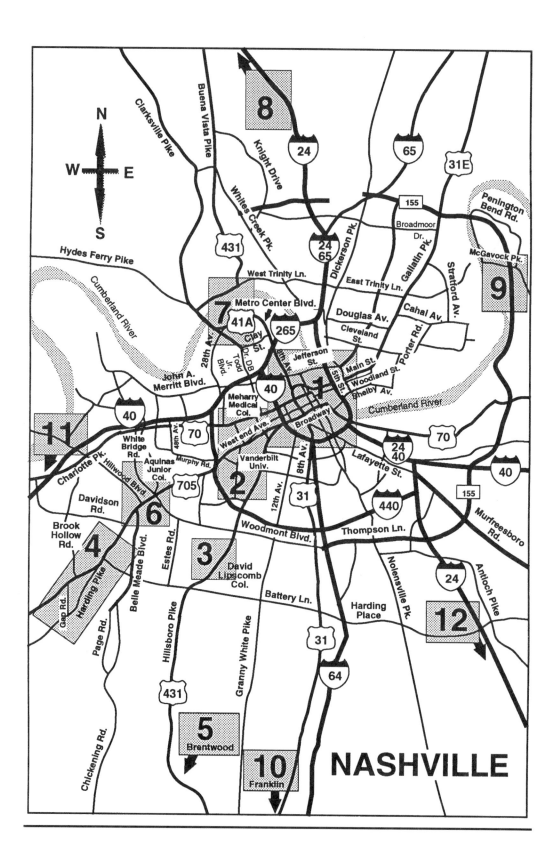

⌂ Restaurant Listings

The following listings offer additional information about the restaurants represented in the recipe sections of this book.

KEY:
Prices/credit cards: $ (under $10); $$ ($10 to $20); $$$ ($20 and up); □ (credit cards accepted); no □ (credit cards not accepted)
Dress: C (casual); D (dressy)
Map locations: (1) Downtown; (2) University Area; (3) Green Hills; (4) Belle Meade; (5) Brentwood; (6) White Bridge Road; (7) Metro Center; (8) North of Nashville; (9) Opryland; (10) Franklin (30 minutes south of downtown Nashville); (11) West of Nashville; (12) Southeast of Nashville

Arnold's Country Kitchen, 605 8th Ave. South, Nashville, TN 37203; (615) 256-4455. This downtown family-owned cafe features freshly prepared Southern-style food. Specialties are roast beef and fresh peach pie. Serves breakfast and lunch Monday through Friday. $; no □; C; (1)

Arthur's in Union Station, 1001 Broadway, Nashville, TN 37203; (615) 255-1494. Located in Nashville's historic train station, the elegant menu here features a fixed-price, six-course dinner for $39.50. Valet parking; reservations suggested; $$$; □; D; (1)

August Moon, Green Hills Court, 4000 Hillsboro Rd., Nashville, TN 37215; (615) 298-9999. An informal neighborhood restaurant featuring Hunan, Mandarin, Szechwan, and Cantonese cuisine. Restful and quiet atmosphere. $; □; C; (3)

Belle Meade Brasserie, 101 Page Rd., Nashville, TN 37205; (615) 356-5450. This smart, upscale bistro serves new American classics, specializing in grilled seafood and poultry. Restaurant is also noted as a mini art gallery; permanent work displayed by local artist Miles Maille. Reservations suggested; $$; □; C and D; (3)

Biddle's Lunch Box, 7101 Executive Center Dr., Brentwood, TN 37027; (615) 370-8565. Housed in the Gatlinburg Building in the Koger Center, this small, super-clean establishment offers freshly made breads, sandwiches, soups, homemade desserts, and hot beverages for lunch Monday through Friday. $; □; C; (5)

Bridge House Tea Room, 136 North 4th Ave., Franklin, TN 37064; (615) 794-7794 or 794-7329. Located in a small historic house with a light and airy courtyard, this Southern tearoom features soups, casseroles, and desserts. Reservations suggested for parties of 6 or more; $; ☐; C; (10)

C & J Diner, 137 7th Ave. North, Nashville, TN 37203, (615) 255-6363; and 405 31st Ave. North, Nashville, TN 37209, (615) 329-1120. Both locations serve breakfast and lunch, and both feature Southern home cooking, such as fried chicken, turnip greens, and mashed potatoes. $; no ☐; C; (1)

Caesar's Ristorante Italiano, Lion's Head Village, 88 White Bridge Rd., Nashville, TN 37205; (615) 352-3661. This small establishment typifies what a neighborhood restaurant in Italy would offer customers—generous servings and a family atmosphere. Specialties are pasta, chicken, and shrimp. Reservations suggested for parties of 8 or more; $$; ☐; C; (6)

Cakewalk Restaurant, 3001 West End Ave., Nashville, TN 37203; (615) 320-7778. Urban and stylish, this creative restaurant offers a blend of classic dishes with unusual combinations. Open for lunch and dinner. Dinner reservations suggested; $$; ☐; C and D; (2)

Cascades, Opryland Hotel, 2800 Opryland Dr., Nashville, TN 37214 (20 minutes from downtown Nashville on I-40 east to Briley Parkway); (615) 889-1000. Breakfast bar, lunch bar, and dinner are served in a relaxing water garden setting. American cuisine such as prime rib, seafood, and Maryland crabmeat soup are specialties. $$; ☐; C; (9)

Choices Restaurant, 108 4th Ave. South, Franklin, TN 37064; (615) 791-0001. In this old restored hardware store, which is on the National Register of Historic Places, customers seated in rooms on various levels are served a menu of eclectic seasonal ingredients. Specialties are salads, house-prepared salad dressings, soups, and desserts. Reservations suggested for parties of 5 or more; $ (lunch) and $$ (dinner); ☐; C; (10)

Clayton-Blackmon Gourmet Deli and Catering Co., 4117 Hillsboro Rd., Nashville, TN 37215; (615) 297-3441. This upscale gourmet carry-out and eat-in combination is bright and airy, fun and unusual. Specialties are home-baked yeast rolls, chicken salad, Greek salad, and chicken pot pie. $; ☐; C; (3)

The Corner Market, Westgate Shopping Center, 6051 Highway 100, Nashville, TN 37205; (615) 352-6772. Attractive gourmet grocery/restaurant/carry-out establishment. Customers are offered soups, sandwiches, salads, and dinners-to-go. Lovers of good gumbo and Cajun fare know to come here. $; ☐ (MasterCard and VISA only); C; (4)

Crown Court Regal, Maxwell House Hotel, 2025 MetroCenter Blvd., Nashville, TN 37228; (615) 259-4343. This attractive restaurant boasts an unmatched view of Nashville from its 10th-floor vantage point. Specialties are pancakes, crispy shrimp, drunken steak, and Szechwan cuisine. Reservations suggested; $$; ☐; C and D; (7)

Dynasty Restaurant, 3415 West End Ave., Nashville, TN 37203; (615) 269-0188. Chinese cuisine is served here in a restful atmosphere. Peking duck, the chef's spicy chicken, and scallops and shrimp in hot garlic sauce are a few of the specialties. $$; ☐; C; (2)

F. Scott's, 2220 Bandywood Dr., Nashville, TN 37215; (615) 269-5861. This is a popular upscale neighborhood bistro specializing in fresh seafood, pasta, and lamb. Serves both lunch and dinner. $$$; ☐; C; (3)

Faison's, 2000 Belcourt Ave., Nashville, TN 37212; (615) 298-2112. A popular upscale restaurant close to Vanderbilt University, this is a fun place to go, and there's always a crowd. The menu is diverse—pasta, broiled meats, fresh salads, and sinful desserts. $$; ☐; C; (2)

Finezza, 5404 Harding Rd., Nashville, TN 37205; (615) 356-9398. This new Italian establishment offers customers a casual trattoria-style atmosphere specializing in classic dishes such as pasta and pizza. White arches, open kitchen, loud and boisterous; this is a good family place. $; ☐; C; (4)

Granite Falls Restaurant, 2000 Broadway, Nashville, TN 37203; (615) 327-9250. Patio dining is popular in this small restaurant. Located close to Vanderbilt University, the ambiance is a mix of casual and formal. Pasta and seafood are the specialties. $$; ☐, C; (2)

Hachland Hill Inn, 1601 Madison St., Clarksville, TN 37043 (1 hour north on I-24 from downtown Nashville); (615) 647-1400. This quaint dining establishment and private home is also a bed and breakfast. Home cooking and gracious hospitality is the specialty. Log cabins on the property are furnished with antiques. Reservations necessary; $$$; ☐; C or D; (8)

Jimmy Kelly's, 217 Louise Ave., Nashville, TN 37203; (615) 329-4349. A favorite with Nashvillians, this quintessential steak house, located in a renovated Victorian mansion, is famous for its New York strip, filet mignon, and blackened catfish. $$$; ☐; C; (2)

Julian's Restaurant Français. (*Editor's note:* Though this grande dame of elegant dining and Dirona Award–winning restaurant closed its doors in the summer of 1992, we are pleased to be able to offer readers several recipes as a delightful reminder of Julian's lovely atmosphere and extensive menu.)

The Mad Platter, 1239 6th Ave. North, Nashville, TN 37208; (615) 242-2563. This unique restaurant, located in a century-old store in a historic Germantown neighborhood, is off the beaten path. The married chef/owners serve upscale gourmet cuisine for lunch and dinner. Imaginative menus, which change weekly, include rack of lamb moutarde, salmon and scallop Wellington, pork tenderloin with apples and brie, and quail with green peppercorn sauce. Dinner reservations necessary; $ (lunch) and $$/$$$ (dinner); □; C; (1)

Mario's, 2005 Broadway, Nashville, TN 37203; (615) 327-3232. One of Music City's oldest and better restaurants. Both the owner and the menu, which features northern Italian cuisine, have attracted national celebrities. Reservations suggested; $$$; □; D; (2)

Merchants, 401 Broadway, Nashville, TN 37203; (615) 254-1892. This elegant white-tablecloth restaurant is located in a restored pre–Civil War downtown hotel close to the Cumberland River. Walls are decorated with old letters and memorabilia found during the restoration. Lunch and dinner are served on the upper floors as well as the street level. Menus are imaginative, with specials including grilled beef, seafood, and poultry. Lunch $ and C, dinner $$/$$$ and D; □; (1)

Mere Bulles, 152 2nd Ave. North, Nashville, TN 37201; (615) 256-1946. This upscale downtown restaurant tucked into a restored vintage warehouse was once used as the roasting plant for Nashville's own Maxwell House coffee. The atmosphere includes exposed brick walls, jazz music, and a look at the Cumberland River. The menu offers contemporary cuisine: grilled steaks, pasta, seafood, veal, and game. $$; □; C to D; (1)

Merridee's Bread Basket, 110 4th Ave. South, Franklin, TN 37064; (615) 790-3755. A renovated brick buggy shop houses this gem. Beamed ceilings, quilts, and baskets lend atmosphere. The owner's Scandinavian background is reflected in the bakery/restaurant menu. Sweet rolls and omelets are served for breakfast; homemade soups, salads, and sandwiches on whole-grain breads appear for lunch. Dessert is from-scratch pies. $; □; C; (10)

Midtown Cafe, 102 19th Ave. South, Nashville, TN 37215; (615) 320-7176. This small establishment off Broadway offers convenient access to the business community, yet parking is no problem. Cozy seating; easy, elegant atmosphere. The menu offers a broad spectrum of American and Continental cuisine. Specialties are seafood, pastas, and veal. $$; credit cards are accepted; C and D; (2)

Miss Mary Bobo's Boarding House, Main St., Lynchburg, TN 37352; (615) 759-7394. Take I-24 south out of Nashville, head for Lynchburg, and 90 minutes later experience a time warp. Locals remember Miss Mary and the tables she set for boarders and lunch guests. Miss Mary's relatives are keeping the tradition alive. Southern dishes, served family style, are legendary—fresh vegetables, Jubilee Shrimp, Intoxicated Chicken, hot breads, rich from-scratch desserts, and much, much more. Lunch reservations necessary; $; ☐; C; (12)

Mosko's Muncheonette, 2204 Elliston Pl., Nashville, TN 37203; (615) 327-3562. An excellent place to order carry-out gourmet made-from-scratch soups, sandwiches, and desserts. Seating is limited, and the atmosphere is casual and fun in this combination lunch and tobacco shop. Specialties are Italian Sausage and Cabbage Soup and Hummingbird Cake. $; ☐; C; (2)

Old Hickory, Opryland Hotel, 2800 Opryland Dr., Nashville, TN 37214 (20 minutes from downtown Nashville on I-40 east to Briley Parkway); (615) 889-1000. Named for President Andrew Jackson, the atmosphere of this restaurant is one of quiet elegance. The menu features Continental cuisine, offering such items as Tennessee rainbow trout, veal Oscar, and beef tournedos. $$$; ☐; D; (9)

Our House, 1059 Haley Rd., Wartrace, TN 37183 (75-minute drive on I-24; get off at Exit 97); (800) 876-6616. Not a restaurant in the true sense, in that the owner renovated his grandmother's house, then decorated it with family treasures before opening as a fine dining establishment. The atmosphere is like entertaining at home; the menu is like eating in the big city. Seafood, lamb, fresh vegetables, and homemade desserts are specialties. $$; ☐; C; (12)

Peking Garden, 1923 Division St., Nashville, TN 37203; (615) 327-2020. Well-prepared Chinese food of different styles is the hallmark of this establishment. The atmosphere is quiet and restful, and the dishes are attractively served. $$; ☐; C and D; (2)

The Picnic, Inc. 4334 Harding Rd., Nashville, TN 37205; (615) 297-5398. Off to itself surrounded by a white picket fence, this small cafe and luncheonette in the back of the Belle Meade Drug Store offers a warm, friendly place to have lunch. Carry-out offered. Fresh chicken salad, muffins, Betty's Brownies, and soups are specialties. $; no ☐; C; (4)

The Pineapple Room at Cheekwood, Forest Park Dr., Nashville, TN 37205; (615) 352-4859. This upscale tearoom is in a beautiful setting looking out onto the well-kept lawns of Cheekwood, the Tennessee Botanical Gardens and Fine Arts Center. The menu features soups, salads, sandwiches, and other lunch specials. Excellent desserts are also served. $$; ☐; C or D; (4)

Plaza Grille, Loew's Vanderbilt Plaza Hotel, 2100 West End Ave., Nashville, TN 37203; (615) 320-1700. This new establishment offers healthful Mediterranean, Eastern Spanish, Southern French, and Northwest Italian cuisine. Grilled foods are featured. $$; ☐; C; (2)

The Puffy Muffin, H.G. Hills Shopping Center, 231 Franklin Rd., Brentwood, TN 37027; (615) 373-2741. The two owners have made this small neighborhood restaurant into a popular, cozy place for friends to meet for lunch. Chicken salad, quiche, and home-baked desserts are specialties. $; ☐; C; (5)

Rainbow Key, Lion's Head Village, 80 White Bridge Rd., Nashville, TN 37205; (615) 352-7252. Landlocked Nashvillians can enjoy coastal dishes, tropical drinks, and a fun Caribbean/Key West atmosphere at this establishment. Coconut shrimp, conch fritters, jerk chicken, and a pie called Tropical Silk are some of the attractions. $$; ☐; C; (6)

Rhett's, Opryland Hotel, 2800 Opryland Dr., Nashville, TN 37214 (20 minutes from downtown Nashville on I-40 east to Briley Parkway); (615) 889-1000. As the name might suggest, this establishment offers a traditional Southern atmosphere for breakfast, lunch, and dinner. Chicken and dumplings (sort of like chicken pot pie) and the Scarlet Salad are big lunch items. White bean soup cooked with ham hock, prime rib, catfish, rainbow trout, and Goo-Goo Pie are popular at dinner. More sophisticated items, like pheasant and lamb chops, are offered, too. $$; ☐; D; (9)

Rotier's, 2413 Elliston Pl., Nashville, TN 37203; (615) 327- 9892. Noted for its cheeseburgers on French bread, rich milkshakes, plate lunches, and nightly dinner specialties, this family-owned and operated neighborhood restaurant has been a favorite of residents and the college crowd for around 30 years. Down-home atmosphere, with lots of local color. $; ☐; C; (2)

Satsuma Tea Room, 417 Union St., Nashville, TN 37219; (615) 256-0760. The energy and pulse of the city, both old and new, can be felt in this downtown tearoom, which has served lunch Monday through Friday to five generations of Nashvillians. Convenient for the business crowd, the cuisine is Southern-style cooking. Specialties are vegetables, salad dressings, homemade breads, and desserts, especially ice cream. $; no ☐; C; (1)

Schwartz's Delicatessen, Belle Meade Plaza, Harding Rd., Nashville, TN 37205; (615) 292-3589. Those who yearn for kosher cold cuts, cheeses, and matzo balls go to Schwartz's, a small neighborhood establishment almost hidden by larger business establishments. Booths offer limited seating space. Great sandwiches, and the chopped liver is made fresh every day. This is Nashville's answer to a New York deli. $; no ☐; C; (4)

The Second Story Cafe, Davis-Kidd Booksellers, 4007 Hillsboro Rd., Nashville, TN 37215; (615) 385-0043. This is an attractive cafe located on the balcony level of one of Nashville's leading bookstores—open, airy, attractive, and upbeat. Customers come to browse for books and meet friends for lunch. Menu includes homemade soups, fresh salads with homemade dressings, and from-scratch desserts. Desserts only are served in the evening. $; ☐; C; (3)

Shadowbrook, 5397 Rawlings Rd., Joelton, TN 37080 (30 minutes from downtown Nashville on I-23 north); (615) 876-0700. This unique, castle-like setting, which was the owner's childhood home, combines art, elegant home-cooked food, and Old South hospitality. Specialties are beef tenderloin, shrimp scampi, and Shadowbrook's Pecan Pie. Reservations a must; $$$; no ☐; D; (8)

Slice of Life, 1811 Division St., Nashville, TN 37203; (615) 329-2525. This combination bakery and restaurant emphasizes healthful, natural, homemade-style foods. Specialties are vegetarian and macrobiotic selections as well as freshly baked goods. $; ☐; C; (2)

Sperry's, 5109 Harding Rd., Nashville, TN 37205; (615) 353-0809. One of Nashville's veteran restaurants, this has long been considered one of the best places to go for outstanding beef. Served in an English pub atmosphere, aged Western beef, rack of lamb, fresh salmon, swordfish, and Alaskan king crab are specialties. $$; ☐; C; (4)

The Stockyard, 901 2nd Ave. North, Nashville, TN 37201; (615) 255-6464. Choice cuts of beef cooked over hickory charcoal are this restaurant's specialty. Located in a turn-of-the-century brick building that once housed offices for the buyers and sellers of the Nashville Union Stockyard, little has changed in the atmosphere except for carpeting, drapery, and wallpaper. Live entertainment is presented nightly in the Bull Pen and the Studio Lounge. $$$; ☐; C; (1)

Sunset Grill, 2001 Belcourt Ave., Nashville, TN 37212; (615) 386-3663. A sophisticated contemporary atmosphere with eclectic California-type cuisine, lamb, veal, fresh seafood, duck, pasta, and beef are the specialties. After 10 p.m., every menu item is half price. $/$$; ☐; C; (2)

32nd Avenue Brasserie, 3201 West End Ave., Nashville, TN 37203; (615) 383-0926. A fireplace, brick walls, local artwork, and a piano player give this establishment a friendly, upbeat atmosphere. Fresh seafood, steaks, chicken, and pasta dishes are the specialties. Convenient to downtown, Hillsboro, and Green Hills. $$; ☐; C; (2)

12th & Porter, 114 12th Ave. North, Nashville, TN 37203; (615) 254-7236. Located behind the *Nashville Banner* and *The Tennessean* newspapers, the atmosphere of this small eatery is funky cinderblock. The menu features dishes like Pasta Ya Ya, BBQ Shrimp, and Hershey Bar Cake—all wonderfully delicious. You have to see it to believe it. $; ☐; C; (1)

The Wild Boar, 2014 Broadway, Nashville, TN 37203; (615) 329-1313. Rustic elegance describes The Wild Boar, with its Southern cuisine featuring wild game, rainbow trout, and sour mash cheesecake. Conveniently located to Vanderbilt University. $$; ☐; C; (2)

🏛 Restaurant Index

Quail Stuffed with Raspberry Barley in Port Wine and Ginger Sauce, 24

Merridee's Bread Basket
Chocolate Chess Pecan Pie, 117
Minnesota Wild Rice Soup, 9
Molasses Sugar Cookies, 135

Midtown Cafe
Midtown Chicken with Mustard Caper Sauce, 77
Scallops en Casserole, 56

Miss Mary Bobo's Boarding House
Boarding House Meatloaf, 94
Farmhouse Country-Fried Steak, 92
Intoxicated Chicken, 79
Jack Daniel's Chocolate Birthday Cake, 126
Jack Daniel's Ice Cream, 101
Jubilee Chocolate Cheesecake, 130
Jubilee Shrimp, 26
Tennessee Berry Crisp, 134

Mosko's Muncheonette
Cold Pasta Salad with Vegetables, 5
Hummingbird Cake with Cream Cheese Frosting, 123
Italian Sausage and Cabbage Soup, 10
Potato Soup, 13

Old Hickory
Asparagus Surprise, 7
Filet of Red Snapper Dieppoise, 65
Jumbo Scampi, 51

Our House
Baked Ocean Perch, 64
Citrus Grilled Tuna, 57
Fresh Blueberry Soup, 16
Grilled Rack of Lamb, 84
Our House Italian Cream Cake, 119
Salmon Loaf with Cucumber Dressing, 61

Peking Garden
Crab Rangoon, 34
Peking Garden Chicken with Lemon Sauce, 75

The Picnic, Inc.
Herbed Baked Chicken Breast, 76
Lemon Squares, 133
Tomato Basil Soup, 15

The Pineapple Room at Cheekwood
Chocolate Chip Pecan Pie, 114
Norwegian Apple Pie with Rum Sauce, 115
Tuscan Tomato Soup, 14

Plaza Grille
Baked Oysters with Crabmeat and Pesto, 31

🏛 Recipe Index

The bold asterisk (*) preceding a recipe title indicates a "recipe within a recipe"; that is, one that appears within the preparation instructions for a primary recipe, but which in some cases could stand alone or be served with another favorite dish.

BEGINNINGS

Quail Stuffed with Raspberry Barley in Port Wine and Ginger Sauce, 24
  *Port Wine and Ginger Sauce, 24
Seafood Rémoulade, 28
Smoked Nova Scotia Salmon with Garnish, 25
Spinach Fritters, 37
Tomato Basil Soup, 15
Treasure of the Sea, 29
Tuscan Tomato Soup, 14

MAIN COURSES

*Angel Hair St. Andrew, 41
Bahama-Que Shrimp, 53
Baked Ocean Perch, 64
Black Jack Filet, 88
Black Linguine with Mussels, 47
Boarding House Meatloaf, 94
Bridge House Chicken Casserole, 69
Broken-Hearted Fettuccine, 46
C & J Diner's Fried Chicken, 81
Caesar's Ziti alla Carbonara, 43
Cherokee Forest Rainbow Trout with Mushrooms and Shrimp, 66
Chicken Breast alla Caesar, 74
Chicken Calypso, 72
Chicken Jerusalem, 80
Citrus Grilled Tuna, 57
Coq au Vin with Herbs, 78
Crawfish Étouffé, 48
Creole Shrimp, 52
Deep-Fried Prawns, 50
Dragon Flower Pork, 96
  *Homemade Brown Sauce, 96
Duck Cordon Bleu with Marinara Sauce, 82
  *Marinara Sauce, 82
Farmhouse Country-Fried Steak, 92
Filet of Red Snapper Dieppoise, 65
Grilled Rack of Lamb, 84
Grilled Swordfish in Ginger-Soy Sauce with Dijon Vegetables and Spoon Rolls, 58
  *Dijon Vegetables, 58
  *Spoon Rolls, 59
Grouper in Corn Husks with Corn Relish and Poblano Cream Sauce, 62
  *Corn Relish, 63
  *Poblano Cream Sauce, 62
Herbed Baked Chicken Breast, 76
Home-Style Deep-Fried Spareribs, 95
Honey-Lemon Chicken, 73

SWEET ENDINGS

■ About the Author

Bernie Wyckoff Arnold, who has served as food editor for both the *Nashville Banner* and *The Tennessean* newspapers, has lived in Nashville since arriving in 1944 to attend David Lipscomb University. During these nearly 50 years she has seen the Nashville restaurant scene grow from a handful of eateries to an extensive and varied list of excellent establishments.

As a food writer and critic who has traveled widely, Bernie has developed a discriminating palate that eminently qualifies her to put together the best in Nashville restaurant food. Her food columns have won numerous awards and she is frequently asked to judge local, regional, and national food contests, including the Pillsbury Bake-Off.

In addition to her newspaper writing, Bernie was home editor of *Nashville Magazine* for eight years and is presently a contributing food writer for the national *Christian Woman Magazine.* She is a member of the Newspaper Food Editors and Writers Association, of The Herb Society of Nashville (a chapter of The Herb Society of America), and formerly of the Society of Professional Journalists.

Bernie is married to Henry Arnold, recently retired college professor and music critic for the *Nashville Banner.* They have four children and four grandchildren.